Pillsbury

savvy
shopper's
cookbook

**Hundreds of simple strategies for smart spending
and inspiring mealtime ideas**

WILEY
Wiley Publishing, Inc.

GENERAL MILLS

Editorial Director: Jeff Nowak

Publishing Manager:
Christine Gray

Manager, Cookbooks: Lois Tlusty

Editor: Grace Wells

Recipe Development and Testing:
Pillsbury Kitchens

Photography: General Mills
Photography Studios and Image
Library

WILEY PUBLISHING, INC.

Publisher: Natalie Chapman

Associate Publisher:
Jessica Goodman

Executive Editor: Anne Ficklen

Editor: Charleen Barila

Senior Production Editor:
Jacqueline Beach

Copyeditor: Kristi Hart

Cover Design: Suzanne Sunwoo

Art director: Tai Blanche

Interior Design and Layout:
Indy Composition Services

Manufacturing Manager:
Kevin Watt

For more great recipes visit
pillsbury.com

Copyright © 2010 by General Mills, Minneapolis, Minnesota. All rights reserved.

Published by John Wiley & Sons, Inc., Hoboken, New Jersey

Published simultaneously in Canada

For general information on our other products and services or for technical support, please contact our Customer Care Department within the United States at (877) 762-2974, outside the United States at (317) 572-3993 or fax (317) 572-4002.

Wiley also publishes its books in a variety of electronic formats. Some content that appears in print may not be available in electronic books. For more information about Wiley products, visit our web site at www.wiley.com.

Library of Congress Cataloging-in-Publication Data:

The savvy shopper's cookbook : hundreds of simple strategies for smart spending and inspiring mealtime ideas.
   p. cm.
 At head of title: Pillsbury
 Includes index.
 ISBN 978-0-470-54397-9 (pbk.)
 1. Low budget cookery. 2. Brand name products. I. Pillsbury Company. II. Title: Pillsbury. III. Title: Pillsbury the savvy shopper's cookbook.
 TX652.S2885 2010
 641.5'52—dc22

                     2009049262

ISBN: 978-0-470-54397-9

Printed in the United States of America

10 9 8 7 6 5 4 3 2

Cover photos: French Dip Sandwiches (page 84); Thai Peanut Chicken and Noodles (page 118); Turkey Gyro Pizza (page 30); Chunky Tomato-Basil Soup (page 180); Mostaccioli with Italian Sausage (page 132); Chunky Beef and Vegetable Chili (page 86); Pulled Pork Sandwiches with Avocado-Onion Slaw (page 102); Asian Salmon (page 140)

Dear Friends,

Cooking for family and friends gives us a great deal of satisfaction and joy, but there can be times when we feel the food budget is being stretched to the max.

Pillsbury Savvy Shopper's Cookbook comes to the rescue and helps put the elastic back into your budget! Every recipe includes cost per serving so you can plan your weekly meals wisely. Check out "Easy Savings" (page 6) for ways to plan, shop and cook to maximize your food dollar.

Let your slow cooker be your pal because you can serve less-expensive cuts of meat more often. Go meatless once or twice a week not only to be cost-effective, but it's also a great way to get grains, beans and more veggies into your family meals.

There are times when we all need a little TLC. Whip up an old-time comfort food such as meat loaf or mac and cheese, which can be cheap and comforting. Or turn your dining room into the "local bistro" and serve up restaurant favorites to make any occasion special and affordable.

So let's be savvy and serve flavor-packed meals every day to keep stretching that food dollar.

Warmly,

Lois Tlusty

& Grace Wells

TABLE OF CONTENTS

Easy $avings   6

1 Stretch the Meat Dollar   12

2 Saved by the Slow Cooker   68

3 Eating Out at Home   108

4 No One Will Miss the Meat   148

5 Snacks To Go or Eat at Home   184

Metric Conversion Guide   222

Index   223

Easy $avings

Food dollars don't go as far as they once did. But big food savings just got a whole lot simpler. There are smart, simple adjustments you can make to your daily routine to make food shopping easier on your wallet without sacrificing delicious, flavorful meals.

It Pays to Plan Ahead

Food Budget? What Food Budget?

You won't realize you're overspending unless you know what you *should* be spending. That means creating a personal food budget that takes your income, location, family size and eating habits into account. Start by going through your financial records, ideally for the last six to twelve months. Determine where you can trim expenses and what you can realistically spend in two categories: groceries and restaurants. *Voilà*—your monthly food budget. Even better, challenge yourself to go below it, as long as you can identify specifically where there's room to trim costs. A little more work up front will save *big* money and time in the long run.

Master the Grocery List

Good news: No need to start a grocery list from scratch every week. Create a master list on your computer, and simply print one out when needed, or keep a stack of them clipped to your refrigerator. Keeping track of what's needed will be easier than ever, and you'll avoid those dreaded last-minute trips to the pricey corner store for the milk you forgot—that's time and money saved.

Let It Grow Include all items you buy regularly, and leave extra space for write-ins. Add recurring write-ins to your master list.

Order, Please Group items in the order you encounter them at the grocery store. Separate them by store if you shop in multiple locations.

Location, Location, Location Keep the list, with pen, in a central spot in the kitchen, such as clipped to the refrigerator. The more convenient it is for household members to mark off items they finish, the more likely they are to follow along with your new plan.

Meal-Planning 101

A little time set aside for weekly meal-planning pays off. No more frustrating last-minute dinner dashes or exasperated takeout splurges for you! Start here, and take it step by step.

Step 1: Make a chart sectioning off daily meals, including snacks and brown-bag lunches. Create a separate section for a grocery list, or if you've created a master list, have that on hand.

Step 2: Scan your refrigerator for what needs to be used, such as leftovers or vegetables that might not last a few more days. Plan immediate meals around them so they don't go to waste.

Price Check!

Keep a small notebook in your bag filled with the prices (and sizes) of the items you buy regularly. The next time a "sale" sticker catches your eye, consult your records to ensure the deal is real. You may be surprised at how often it isn't.

Step 3: Fill in the rest of the week, adding needed recipe ingredients to the grocery list as you go. Be sure to check your coupons for expiration dates and account for those in your meal plan. Add night-before prep time to your plan, too.

Step 4: Take a final assessment, making sure you've realistically considered the week's activities and the time you'll have to prepare each meal.

Smart Shopping

Preparation is key here—the more you plan ahead, the easier and more efficient your shopping trip will be.

Schedule Give yourself a better shot at the ideal grocery-shopping trip by planning to go solo, during off-peak hours, with plenty of browsing time. Being distracted, crowded or rushed encourages impulse purchases.

BYOB Bring your own *bags*, that is. Many stores offer a reusable bag discount, so keep a stash handy.

Clip Not a "coupon person"? Try committing to weekly coupon sessions before planning your meals. Scan circulars or the Internet (search "grocery coupons" for popular sites). On or offline, look for specials at your favored stores. Your first coupon-plus-sale savings could change your mind.

Withdraw Take out just enough cash to cover your budgeted groceries. Paying in real dollars discourages shopping off-list.

Do the Math

A good buy starts with one key equation: Unit price per ounce. Take the time to make some quick comparison calculations before tossing anything into the cart. Remember, sale prices and larger packages do not an automatic bargain make. For example:

$$\$2.99 \div 16 \text{ oz.} = 19 \text{ cents per unit}$$

Shop Smart

Close-to-Home Grown

When purchasing meat and produce, your freshest bets appear closest to the farm. Luckily, cutting out middle men typically cuts cost, too. Follow these tips for unearthing the best in farm-fresh goods.

Become a Farmers'-Market Regular No doubt it's fresh, in season and grown or raised nearby. It's also likely to be handed to you by the person who cared for it. Tip: Try bartering at day's end. Some farmers would rather give a discount than truck items back to the farm and risk waste.

Consider a CSA With Community Supported Agriculture (CSA) programs, consumers buy "shares" of local farms in the form of a box of fresh-picked seasonal produce weekly, all harvest-season long. Two caveats: You'll probably have to invest up front for the entire season, and each week's amount and variety rely solely on Mother Nature. Consider splitting a share with a friend or two. Find one at www.localharvest.org.

Cultivate Your Inner Farmer Container gardening is a budget-friendly way to raise some of your own produce, from a few small pots of herbs on the window sill to tomatoes in a big planter out back. You can't get any fresher—or less expensive—than home grown!

Super Market Skills

Check out these in-store tactics to help you stick to your list and your budget.

Shop Seasonally You'll net the freshest food at the best prices.

Thin Is In It's the best-sized slice for stretching deli meats and cheeses.

Stray Smart Go ahead and check the discount shelves. Just don't go off-list based on what you find.

Hunt High & Low Look beyond eye level for deals lurking out of your sight line.

Good Timing Check expiration dates—especially on sale items and those with a short shelf life.

Don't Go There Have a confirmed weakness?
Skip your "danger" aisle (or aisles) to avoid temptation.

Home Store

When looking for organizational accessories, first search under your own roof. Leftover food containers, such as butter tubs or baby-food jars, could house bulk spices or snacks instead. Search outside the kitchen, too. That office tote or clear plastic shoe drawer, for example, could make a portable snack bin or corral half-used bags and boxes of pasta in your pantry. If you decide you must buy, pinpoint the exact function and size of the organizational product you require. A hasty purchase wastes money and space.

Buying in Bulk

The two kinds of bulk buying offer any budget seeker a big score with low cost per unit. Choose the type that best fits your unique household to prevent wasted food (and money).

1. Bulk in Quantity Purchasing in quantity can save money, but be sure you like the item enough that it will be consumed before the expiration date. Take an honest look at your available storage space, too, so you have a place to tuck everything away.

2. Bulk in Bins Scoop yourself to personalize the amount, whether it's enough to fill up a favorite bulk pasta container or just a recipe's worth of a rarely used spice.

Money or Time?

Which is the best buy: bone-in or boneless chicken, whole or shredded carrots, dried or refrigerated pasta? Boneless chicken may be more convenient, but bone-in chicken costs less per pound. And after you remove the bones, fat and skin, you'll have the same edible portion as boneless but for less money!

Simple Kitchen Solutions

Order, Order

Tired of searching for that item you *just knew you had here somewhere* only to stumble across an unexpected arsenal of ketchup or last week's leftovers languishing in the back of the fridge? Apply these organizational rules to your refrigerator, freezer and cupboards to eliminate wasted time, food and money.

Group Like with Like Consider the way your family most often uses each item. Mayo, for example, could find a home with the other condiments, or in a bin containing sandwich necessities.

Use Prime Real Estate Well Reserve the front-and-center spot of any space for items accessed most often. Hard-to-reach storage, particularly very high or very low, should contain things used less frequently.

Label with Abandon Leave zero question as to what things are and where they live. Whether you use a label maker or masking tape and a marker, leave no shelf or container a mystery.

Incoming!

Don't waste a minute worrying about food waste and missing expiration dates. Just follow these simple steps while putting away your groceries.

Clean Create a fresh start with a quick tidy of the fridge, freezer and pantry before your shopping trip.

Prep Make fruits and vegetables ready to use or eat by washing and thoroughly drying them before storing. Consider chopping and dividing them as well, when appropriate.

Rotate Place newer goods, whether in the pantry, fridge or freezer, behind older ones. What you see first is always what should be used next.

Contain Place any raw or defrosting meats or poultry in the coldest zone of your refrigerator on an edged tray, far from produce, to prevent bacterial contamination.

The Winner is You

About to dial for takeout? Instead, declare a Pantry Cook-Off. Give yourself and any other helpers in the house five minutes to scour the kitchen for the ingredients you've been overlooking—you know they're there!—and design a one-pan game plan. You'll have dinner on the table faster than delivery, no tip necessary.

Hot Dish, Cool Tip

Line your casserole pan with foil before assembling the ingredients. Make as usual, freeze, then remove it from the dish, foil and all, and seal it in an extra-large freezer plastic bag. Return it to the original pan to thaw, and bake as directed.

Creative Cost-Cutting

Love Those Leftovers

Yesterday's scraps or a head start on today's new meal? Rework the way you consider and care for leftovers for original meals and zero waste.

Dedicated Space Label and date all leftovers, and store them in just one designated spot. Rotate, putting recent food behind existing items.

Total Makeover Soup easily turns into a casserole base, and fajitas can fill a Mexican omelet. Get creative!

Mix-n-Match The meat from that half of a restaurant-lunch steak sandwich plus last night's side of peas could mingle well in a salad or a stir-fry.

Love It More Later Enjoy the leftover as-is? Portion and freeze it immediately. You'll better appreciate it as a quick-and-simple lunch or dinner down the road.

Party o' Plenty

Meal planning and diversification go social with do-it-yourself frozen-meal swaps.

Decide on Specific Food Type and Amount Four half-casseroles? Five main dishes for four? Six quarts of soup? Select your standard.

Plan for Fun Have a short BYOB happy hour first. Throw in inexpensive door prizes, such as reusable shopping bags or vintage cookbooks. Make time for each swapper to describe his or her dish.

Swap Well If you didn't plan a one-for-one trade all around, draw numbers for choosing order. Continue in rounds until all the food is allotted.

Go Big Batch

Experiment with bulk cooking for hassle-free meals a day, week or month at a time. It's the perfect use for budget-friendly bulk-bought ingredients, and that ready-to-heat meal will take the place of a last-minute restaurant splurge on nights when nobody feels like cooking.

Start Small Make two of a dish. Eat one, freeze one. Or, for just one week, concentrate on breakfast, lunch or dinner only.

Prep Like Ingredients For every dish, prep all at once. It saves time and makes cleanup easier.

Label Well Include both the date packaged and cooking directions.

Shop One Day, Cook Another Fun and productive is way better than exhausting and overwhelming, right?

Cold Crusader

Think of your freezer as your kitchen's superhero. It saves on-sale items, make-ahead meals and fresh ingredients until you need them. Use its power wisely.

Freeze, Please Keep your freezer set at 0°F for maximum food quality and storage life.

Bins and Bags Use large plastic storage bins as drawers to corral abundant small bags.

Shelf Help Freezer shelf life varies from one month to one year, depending on the food. Find a chart online at www.USDA.gov, and keep it in the kitchen for reference.

Cube It Reserve an ice cube tray for items such as tomato paste, lemon juice, broth and pesto. Once frozen, place cubes in a labeled container for single use.

Just Right Use only containers made for the freezer. Double-bagging doesn't cut it!

No Go These items don't freeze well: custards, cooked eggs, mayo, milk, cream, small chunks of pasta or cooked potato, and watery vegetables such as lettuce.

Using One-Time Ingredients

It's fun to try new recipes, but sometimes you end up with an ingredient or two that's called for in only one recipe. What do you do with the remainder of those one-time ingredients? Here are some suggestions to make the most of your purchases.

Creamy Horseradish Sauce Serve with roast beef, steaks or hamburgers, use as a sandwich spread or add to mashed potatoes.

Crumbled Feta Sprinkle on salads, sliced tomatoes, pizza, pasta dishes, lamb or cooked green vegetables. For an inexpensive appetizer, sprinkle with olive oil and chopped oregano leaves.

Fish Sauce Add a pungent flavor to stir fries, curry dishes and soups, or toss with cooked noodles, rice or vegetables. Use in moderation because of its intense, salty flavor. As a guideline, substitute 1 tablespoon fish sauce for 1 tablespoon soy sauce.

Hoisin Sauce Add a sweet, salty and spicy flavor to marinades, dipping sauces and stir-fry dishes. Use as a basting sauce on chicken or pork during cooking.

Oyster Sauce Add a piquant flavor to marinades, dipping sauces and stir-fry dishes. Toss with cooked noodles, rice or vegetables. Brush on beef, chicken or pork before cooking. Use sparingly because it is salty.

Red Wine Vinegar Use in salad dressings and marinades for meat. After cooking bean, lentil or vegetable soup, add a splash or two to enhance the flavors.

Rice Vinegar Use in place of cider or white vinegar in recipes such as salad dressings, marinades for meat, chicken, seafood or vegetables, or in sauces such as barbecue, teriyaki or sweet-and-sour.

Salsa Verde Serve as a tangy, zesty dip with chips; use in place of tomato salsa on tacos, enchiladas and burritos; or toss with cooked rice or noodles as a side dish. Stir into mayonnaise for a sandwich spread or into chicken or seafood salad sandwich filling.

Stir-Fry Sauce Use in marinades for seafood, chicken or vegetables. Add to a chicken or shellfish salad, or toss with hot cooked rice.

Sweet-and-Sour Sauce Add to chicken, seafood and vegetable stir-fry dishes, use in salad dressing or toss with cooked vegetables.

Teriyaki Marinade and Sauce Add a rich flavor to marinades for meat, chicken or seafood, or use as a dipping sauce. Coat meat or chicken with sauce, and let marinade for a few minutes before cooking.

Rotisserie Chicken— Cooked and Ready to Go

A rotisserie chicken sometimes can be your best price value. Watch for a sale, or purchase them where you get the best price per pound. From a 2-pound chicken, you'll get approximately the following amount of cut-up meat:

Whole chicken . . . . . 3 cups

Breast meat only . . . 2 cups

Dark meat only . . . . 1 cup

CHAPTER 1

Stretch the Meat Dollar

What's better than a fantastic deal that manages to feel indulgent? These recipes master that magic combo, pairing budget-friendly meats with veggies, rice and other welcome meal extenders. Together they create proof positive that less can definitely—and deliciously—taste like more.

Cheap Meats

Follow these grocery-store tips to pay less for your protein.

FLEXIBLE

Be Flexible Have a specific fish or cut of meat on your list, but spy a different-but-similar one on sale? Go ahead. Make that last-minute switch. If you're unsure that it's a good substitute, ask your butcher or fishmonger. This is one instance when going off-list pays.

STOCK UP

Stock Up Don't shell out for individual packaging. Buy the extra-large packages of beef, poultry and seafood—you can repackage appropriately at home if need be. Some items, such as shrimp and meatballs, even come in resealable freezer plastic bags.

SMART

Stew Smart Need stew meat and considering the pre-cut? First, look for the cheapest, leanest cut in the prepackaged meat cooler or the butcher counter. If it beats the price of pre-cut, cube it yourself.

Shop Local

Everything's cheapest when bought straight from the source. Whether it's farm fields or oceans that populate your state, ferret out the most direct connection for meat, poultry or fish. Ask friends, look online or label-read for great deals, as fresh as they come. Bonus: Grocery shopping doubles as a day trip.

Switch to Save

Don't discriminate against those meat, poultry and seafood offerings that consistently bear a low price tag. Pair them with the right recipe and cooking style, and wow! You've craftily satisfied your champagne tastes on a beer budget. Check out this chart to help you experiment with those less expensive offerings.

INGREDIENT	TOP $$	TRY
BEEF	loin, rib eye, porterhouse	brisket, flank steak, skirt steak
CHICKEN	breast	leg, thigh, wing
FISH	salmon, tuna	cod, skate, snapper, sole, tilapia
LAMB	loin	leg, shank, sirloin
PORK	baby back ribs, tenderloin	chops, shoulder, spareribs

Alfredo Chicken Pasta

Creamy Alfredo sauce, veggies and chicken make this pasta dish a family favorite.

Prep Time: 25 Minutes | **Start to Finish:** 25 Minutes | 5 servings

8 oz uncooked bow tie (farfalle) pasta (4 cups)

1 ½ cups frozen sweet peas

2 small carrots, shredded (1 cup)

1 tablespoon vegetable oil

1 lb boneless skinless chicken breasts, cut into thin bite-size strips

1 jar (16 oz) Alfredo pasta sauce

2 teaspoons dried basil leaves

$**1.95** *per serving*

1 In 4-quart Dutch oven, cook pasta as directed on package, adding peas and carrots during last 5 minutes of cooking. Drain; return to Dutch oven.

2 Meanwhile, in 10-inch nonstick skillet, heat oil over medium heat. Add chicken; cook 9 to 11 minutes, stirring frequently, until chicken is no longer pink in center.

3 Stir chicken, Alfredo sauce and basil into pasta mixture in Dutch oven. Cook and stir over medium heat until hot.

1 Serving: Calories 530; Total Fat 24g (Saturated Fat 9g; Trans Fat 0g); Cholesterol 135mg; Sodium 690mg; Total Carbohydrate 48g (Dietary Fiber 5g) **Exchanges:** 3 Starch, 3 Lean Meat, 3 Fat **Carbohydrate Choices:** 3

$mart $avings

Growing herbs? Use 2 tablespoons fresh basil leaves, chopped, for the dried basil. Or use other fresh herbs, such as thyme, oregano or rosemary, for the basil. Check the pantry for other short-cut pasta, such as penne, rotini pasta or medium shells, for the bow tie.

Chicken Potato Nugget Casserole

This kid-pleasing casserole will soon be a family favorite with its creamy chicken and bumpy potato nugget top.

Prep Time: 10 Minutes | **Start to Finish:** 1 Hour 5 Minutes | 4 servings

- 1 can (10 ¾ oz) condensed cream of chicken soup
- 1 cup milk
- 1 tablespoon dried minced onion
- 2 cups cut-up cooked chicken
- 2 cups frozen mixed vegetables, thawed
- 1 bag (16 oz) frozen potato nuggets
- ½ cup shredded American-Cheddar cheese blend (2 oz)

$**1.94** *per serving*

1 Heat oven to 375°F. In ungreased 2-quart casserole, mix soup, milk, dried minced onion, chicken and mixed vegetables. Arrange potato nuggets over top.

2 Bake uncovered 40 to 45 minutes. Sprinkle with cheese. Bake 5 to 10 minutes longer or until bubbly and cheese is melted.

1 Serving: Calories 610; Total Fat 28g (Saturated Fat 12g; Trans Fat 4.5g); Cholesterol 85mg; Sodium 1720mg; Total Carbohydrate 57g (Dietary Fiber 8g) **Exchanges:** 2 ½ Starch, 1 Other Carbohydrate, 1 Vegetable, 3 ½ Lean Meat, 3 Fat **Carbohydrate Choices:** 4

Beef Potato Nugget Casserole: Substitute 1 lb ground beef, cooked and drained, for the 2 cups cooked chicken.

$mart $avings

Dried minced onion is handy to have on the shelf, but you can use ¼ cup chopped onion instead. If you have other vegetables in the freezer, use 2 cups cut green beans, corn or peas, thawed, for the mixed vegetables. American-Cheddar cheese blend adds a nice color, but any shredded cheese will melt nicely and add flavor.

Skillet Chicken Pot Pie

This skillet pot pie is like a taste of the South with its chicken and gravy, topped with flaky biscuits.

Prep Time: 45 Minutes | **Start to Finish:** 45 Minutes | 6 servings

1 tablespoon vegetable oil

1 1/4 lb boneless skinless chicken breasts, cut into 1-inch pieces

1 teaspoon salt

1 1/2 teaspoons dried thyme leaves

1/8 teaspoon pepper

2 cups sliced fresh carrots (4 medium)

2 cups frozen southern-style diced hash brown potatoes (from 32-oz bag)

1 jar (12 or 15 oz) chicken gravy

1 cup frozen sweet peas

1 can (12 oz) refrigerated buttermilk flaky biscuits or flaky biscuits

1/2 teaspoon garlic powder

$**1.77** *per serving*

1 In 12-inch nonstick ovenproof skillet, heat oil over medium-high heat. Add chicken; sprinkle with salt, 1/2 teaspoon of the thyme and the pepper. Cook 5 minutes, stirring frequently, until chicken is browned.

2 Move chicken to one side of skillet. Add carrots and potatoes; cook 5 minutes, stirring frequently. Stir gravy into chicken and vegetables. Heat to boiling. Reduce heat to low. Cover; simmer 20 to 25 minutes, stirring occasionally and adding peas during last 5 minutes of cook time, until chicken is no longer pink in center and vegetables are tender.

3 During last 15 minutes of cook time, heat oven to 400°F. Separate dough into 10 biscuits. Cut each into quarters; place in large bowl. Sprinkle garlic powder and remaining 1 teaspoon thyme over dough; toss to coat. Place on ungreased cookie sheet.

4 Bake 8 to 10 minutes or until biscuit pieces are golden brown. Scatter biscuit pieces over top of cooked chicken mixture before serving.

1 Serving: Calories 450; Total Fat 16g (Saturated Fat 3.5g; Trans Fat 2.5g); Cholesterol 60mg; Sodium 1430mg; Total Carbohydrate 47g (Dietary Fiber 3g) **Exchanges:** 2 1/2 Starch, 1/2 Other Carbohydrate, 1 Vegetable, 2 1/2 Lean Meat, 1 1/2 Fat **Carbohydrate Choices:** 3

$mart $avings

If you have a bag of frozen mixed vegetables in the freezer, use 3 cups mixed vegetables, thawed, for the carrots and peas. After cooking the potatoes, add the mixed veggies with the chicken. Cubed hash brown potatoes are called "southern-style," and shredded potatoes are called "country-style." Either one can be used in this skillet pot pie.

White
Chicken Chili

White chili—usually made with white beans, chicken and chiles instead of red beans, beef and tomatoes—is still packed with plenty of spicy chili flavor.

Prep Time: 30 Minutes | **Start to Finish:** 30 Minutes | 9 servings

1 tablespoon vegetable oil

1 large onion, chopped (1 cup)

2 cloves garlic, finely chopped

1 lb boneless skinless chicken breasts, cut into bite-size pieces

5 ¼ cups chicken broth (from two 32-oz cartons)

2 cans (15 oz each) cannellini beans, drained

2 cans (4.5 oz each) chopped green chiles, drained

1 teaspoon dried oregano leaves

½ teaspoon ground cumin

Dash ground red pepper (cayenne), if desired

1 ½ cups shredded Monterey Jack cheese (6 oz), if desired

Chopped fresh cilantro, if desired

$**1.58** *per serving*

1 In 4-quart Dutch oven, heat oil over medium-high heat until hot. Add onion, garlic and chicken; cook and stir until chicken is no longer pink in center.

2 Stir in remaining ingredients except cheese and cilantro. Heat to boiling. Reduce heat to low; simmer 10 to 15 minutes to blend flavors, stirring occasionally. Serve with cheese and cilantro.

1 Serving (1 cup each): Calories 200; Total Fat 4.5g (Saturated Fat 1g; Trans Fat 0g); Cholesterol 30mg; Sodium 710mg; Total Carbohydrate 20g (Dietary Fiber 5g) **Exchanges:** 1 Starch, ½ Vegetable, 2 ½ Very Lean Meat, ½ Fat **Carbohydrate Choices:** 1

$mart $avings

Stock up on chicken breasts when they're on sale because you'll be making this chili often for family and friends. If ground turkey is on sale, you may want to use a pound instead of the chicken breast. You can add more kick by increasing the amount of ground red pepper—or pass the red pepper sauce at the table!

Chicken-Rice
Burritos

Turn leftover chicken into simple and hearty burritos by adding a few extras that will satisfy even the hungriest stomach!

Prep Time: 20 Minutes | **Start to Finish:** 50 Minutes | 4 servings

2 cups chunky-style salsa

1 cup water

1 cup uncooked instant white rice

1 1/2 cups shredded cooked chicken

1 cup shredded Cheddar cheese (4 oz)

1/2 teaspoon garlic powder

1 package (11 oz) flour tortillas for burritos (8 tortillas; 8 inch)

Shredded lettuce, if desired

Chopped tomatoes, if desired

$2.23 *per serving*

1 Heat oven to 375°F. In 2-quart saucepan, heat salsa and water to boiling. Stir in rice. Cover; remove from heat. Let stand 5 minutes.

2 Stir chicken, cheese and garlic powder into rice mixture. Spoon 1/2 cup chicken-rice mixture onto center of each tortilla. Fold bottom 1/3 of tortilla over filling; fold in sides toward center, leaving top open. Place seam side down in ungreased 13×9-inch (3-quart) glass baking dish.

3 Cover tightly with foil; bake 20 to 30 minutes or until hot. Top with lettuce and tomatoes.

1 Serving (2 burritos each): Calories 610; Total Fat 22g (Saturated Fat 9g; Trans Fat 2.5g); Cholesterol 75mg; Sodium 1960mg; Total Carbohydrate 73g (Dietary Fiber 0g) **Exchanges:** 3 1/2 Starch, 1 1/2 Other Carbohydrate, 2 1/2 Lean Meat, 2 1/2 Fat **Carbohydrate Choices:** 5

Beef-Rice Burritos: Substitute 1 1/2 cups shredded cooked beef or 3/4 lb ground beef, cooked and drained, for the chicken.

Pork-Rice Burritos: Substitute 1 1/2 cups shredded cooked pork for the chicken and 1 cup shredded taco-flavored cheese for the Cheddar cheese.

$mart $avings

Watch for deli rotisserie chickens on sale to use for the cooked chicken. You can shred the chicken while the rice cooks. Have extra cooked rice in the refrigerator? Use 2 cups cooked rice for the instant rice and water. Heat the cooked rice and salsa until hot before adding the other ingredients.

Cheesy Chicken-Tortilla Lasagna

Next time you serve lasagna, surprise the family with a Mexican version using tortillas instead of pasta—they will love it!

Prep Time: 40 Minutes | **Start to Finish:** 1 Hour 35 Minutes | 8 servings

1   can (10 oz) enchilada sauce

2   large tomatoes, chopped (2 cups)

2   cups cubed cooked chicken

8   medium green onions, finely chopped ($\frac{1}{2}$ cup)

1   can (15 oz) black beans, drained, rinsed

1   cup southwest ranch veggie dip (from 15 to 16-oz container)

8   corn tortillas (6 inch), cut in half

1 $\frac{1}{2}$ cups shredded Mexican cheese blend (6 oz)

$\frac{1}{4}$ cup sliced ripe olives, if desired

2   tablespoons chopped fresh cilantro, if desired

$1.92 *per serving*

1   Heat oven to 375°F. Spray 13×9-inch (3-quart) glass baking dish with cooking spray. Spread 2 tablespoons of the enchilada sauce in bottom of baking dish.

2   In medium bowl, mix tomatoes, chicken, onions and beans. In another medium bowl, mix remaining enchilada sauce and the veggie dip until well blended.

3   Arrange 8 tortilla pieces over sauce in dish, overlapping as necessary. Spoon half of the chicken mixture over tortillas; sprinkle with $\frac{1}{2}$ cup of the cheese. Spoon half of the sauce mixture over cheese. Repeat layers once, reserving $\frac{1}{2}$ cup cheese.

4   Cover with foil. Bake 40 to 45 minutes or until hot. Sprinkle with reserved $\frac{1}{2}$ cup cheese. Bake uncovered about 5 minutes longer or until cheese is melted. Let stand 5 minutes before serving. Sprinkle with olives and cilantro.

1 Serving: Calories 420; Total Fat 24g (Saturated Fat 5g; Trans Fat 0g); Cholesterol 75mg; Sodium 620mg; Total Carbohydrate 30g (Dietary Fiber 7g) **Exchanges:** 1 $\frac{1}{2}$ Starch, $\frac{1}{2}$ Other Carbohydrate, 2 $\frac{1}{2}$ Lean Meat, 3 Fat **Carbohydrate Choices:** 2

$mart $avings

If tomatoes aren't juicy and flavorful, use 4 medium plum (Roma) tomatoes instead. If you want to save some money and the environment, place a cookie sheet on top of the baking dish rather than covering with foil. Use the remaining veggie dip for lunch with some crisp veggies, such as carrot, celery, zucchini or jicama sticks.

Summer Chicken Soup with Biscuit Dumplings

A flavorful chicken soup is a great way to use fresh summer vegetables from the farmers' market or your own garden. Serve with cut-up fresh fruit, if desired.

Prep Time: 35 Minutes | **Start to Finish:** 50 Minutes | 6 servings

Soup

- 1 tablespoon vegetable oil
- 1 medium onion, chopped (½ cup)
- 2 cloves garlic, finely chopped
- 1 carton (32 oz) chicken broth
- 12 ready-to-eat baby-cut carrots, cut in half lengthwise
- 4 cups shredded cooked chicken
- 1 medium zucchini, cubed
- 1 medium yellow squash, cubed
- 1 box (9 oz) frozen baby sweet peas, thawed
- ½ teaspoon salt
- ¼ teaspoon pepper
- ¼ cup chopped fresh dill weed

Dumplings

- 1 can (10.2 oz) large refrigerated flaky biscuits (5 biscuits)
- ¼ cup chopped fresh parsley

$2.69 *per serving*

1 In 4-quart saucepan, heat oil over medium-high heat. Cook and stir onion and garlic in oil about 2 minutes or until onion is tender.

2 Add broth; heat to boiling. Add carrots; reduce heat to medium. Cook about 5 minutes or until carrots are tender. Add remaining soup ingredients; increase heat to high. Heat to boiling. Reduce heat to medium-high. Cover; cook 2 to 3 minutes or until vegetables are crisp-tender.

3 Cut biscuits into quarters. Dip one side of each biscuit piece in parsley. Drop biscuits, parsley side up, onto hot soup. Reduce heat to medium. Cover; cook 10 to 15 minutes or until dumplings are no longer doughy in center.

1 Serving (1 ½ cups each): Calories 400; Total Fat 14g (Saturated Fat 3g; Trans Fat 3g); Cholesterol 75mg; Sodium 1340mg; Total Carbohydrate 32g (Dietary Fiber 3g) **Exchanges:** 2 Starch, 1 Vegetable, 4 Lean Meat **Carbohydrate Choices:** 2

$mart $avings

Try different combinations of vegetables, such as green beans and squash, or carrots, parsnips and peas. Parsley adds color to the biscuit dumplings, but if you don't have any, go ahead and make the dumplings without it.

Chicken-Ramen Soup

Chicken-flavor ramen noodle soup mix is embellished with add-ins to enhance the flavor and make a heartier soup that may well become a new family favorite.

Prep Time: 30 Minutes | **Start to Finish:** 45 Minutes | 6 servings

1 tablespoon olive oil

2 medium carrots, cut into
¼-inch slices (1 cup)

2 medium stalks celery, cut into
¼-inch slices (1 cup)

1 medium onion, chopped (½ cup)

2 cloves garlic, finely chopped

2 cups cut-up cooked chicken

6 cups water

1 package (3 oz) chicken-flavor
ramen noodle soup mix

¼ teaspoon salt

¼ teaspoon pepper

$0.71 *per serving*

1 In 5-quart Dutch oven, heat oil over medium heat. Add carrots, celery, onion and garlic; cook 3 to 4 minutes, stirring frequently, until tender.

2 Stir in chicken, water, contents of seasoning packet from soup mix, salt and pepper. Heat to boiling over high heat. Reduce heat to medium; simmer uncovered 10 to 15 minutes.

3 Break apart noodles, stir into soup; simmer uncovered about 3 minutes longer or until noodles are tender.

1 Serving: Calories 190; Total Fat 9g (Saturated Fat 2g; Trans Fat 1g); Cholesterol 40mg; Sodium 600mg; Total Carbohydrate 14g (Dietary Fiber 2g) **Exchanges:** ½ Starch, ½ Other Carbohydrate, 2 Lean Meat, ½ Fat **Carbohydrate Choices:** 1

Beef-Ramen Soup: Substitute 1 lb ground beef for the chicken and beef-flavor ramen noodle soup mix for the chicken-flavor. Cook the beef with the vegetables in step 1 until the beef is brown; drain. Continue as directed in step 2.

$mart $avings

Stock up on ramen noodle soup mix when it's on sale. If you have a leftover cooked veggie—green beans, broccoli or corn—add it to the soup with the noodles or use it instead of the carrots or the celery.

Turkey Gyro Pizza

Some of the delicious flavors of a Greek gyro—garlic, cucumber, tomato, onion and feta cheese—top this cheesy homemade pizza.

Prep Time: 20 Minutes | **Start to Finish:** 35 Minutes | 8 servings

1   can (12 oz) refrigerated classic pizza crust

½   lb lean (at least 90%) ground turkey

2   cloves garlic, finely chopped

½   teaspoon dried oregano leaves

¼   teaspoon salt

½   cup sour cream

1½   cups shredded mozzarella cheese (6 oz)

½   medium cucumber, coarsely chopped (¾ cup)

1   medium tomato, coarsely chopped (¾ cup)

4   thin slices red onion

½   cup crumbled feta cheese

$1.25 *per serving*

1   Heat oven to 425°F. Spray 13×9-inch pan with cooking spray. Unroll dough; press in bottom and slightly up sides of pan to form crust. Bake about 7 minutes or until crust just begins to turn brown on edges.

2   Meanwhile, in 6-inch skillet, cook turkey and garlic over medium-high heat 5 to 7 minutes, stirring occasionally, until turkey is no longer pink. Stir in oregano and salt.

3   Spread sour cream over warm crust. Sprinkle with 1 cup of the mozzarella cheese. Evenly top with cooked turkey. Sprinkle with cucumber and tomato. Separate red onion into rings; arrange over tomato. Sprinkle with remaining ½ cup mozzarella cheese and the feta cheese.

4   Bake 13 to 14 minutes or until edges of crust are golden brown and cheese is melted.

1 Serving: Calories 290; Total Fat 12g (Saturated Fat 7g; Trans Fat 0g); Cholesterol 50mg; Sodium 670mg; Total Carbohydrate 27g (Dietary Fiber 1g) **Exchanges:** 1 Low-Fat Milk, 2 Vegetable, 1 Lean Meat, 1 Fat **Carbohydrate Choices:** 2

Beef Gyro Pizza: Substitute ½ lb lean (at least 80%) ground beef for the turkey.

$mart $avings

Ground turkey is an inexpensive substitute for ground beef. It works well in dishes where other flavors predominate over the meat. You can use plain yogurt rather than the sour cream if you like.

Everyday Lasagna Skillet

Get the same great flavors of baked lasagna in a skillet that is easier to prepare—let one of the kids make it for dinner.

Prep Time: 40 Minutes | **Start to Finish:** 55 Minutes | 6 servings

1   lb lean (at least 80%) ground beef

½   lb bulk mild Italian sausage

1   jar (26 oz) tomato pasta sauce

1   cup water

5   uncooked lasagna noodles, broken into 2-inch pieces

1   container (12 oz) cottage cheese

½   cup grated Parmesan cheese

1   tablespoon dried parsley leaves, if desired

1   egg

1½   cups shredded Italian cheese blend (6 oz)

$2.07 *per serving*

1   In 12-inch nonstick skillet, cook beef and sausage over medium-high heat 5 to 7 minutes, stirring occasionally, until thoroughly cooked; drain. Stir in pasta sauce, water and uncooked noodles. Reduce heat to medium-low. Cover; cook 20 to 25 minutes, stirring occasionally, until pasta is almost tender.

2   Meanwhile, in small bowl, mix cottage cheese, Parmesan cheese, parsley and egg. Spread over partially cooked pasta mixture. Sprinkle with shredded Italian cheese. Cover; cook 10 to 15 minutes longer or until cottage cheese mixture is set and pasta is tender.

1 Serving: Calories 640; Total Fat 34g (Saturated Fat 15g; Trans Fat 1g); Cholesterol 150mg; Sodium 1550mg; Total Carbohydrate 40g (Dietary Fiber 3g) **Exchanges:** 1 ½ Starch, 1 Other Carbohydrate, 5 ½ Medium-Fat Meat, 1 Fat **Carbohydrate Choices:** 2 ½

$mart $avings

There are usually some broken pieces of lasagna noodles in the bottom of the box, so be sure to use them for part of the noodles. And you can use mozzarella cheese for the blend if you prefer. If your family likes spicy food, try hot Italian sausage in this recipe.

Biscuit Cheeseburger Casserole

This has the flavor of a cheeseburger, but rather than being served in a burger bun, it's topped with freshly baked biscuits.

Prep Time: 15 Minutes | **Start to Finish:** 35 Minutes | 5 servings

- 1   lb lean (at least 80%) ground beef
- 1   small onion, chopped (¼ cup)
- ½   small bell pepper (any color), chopped (¼ cup)
- 1   can (8 oz) tomato sauce
- ¼   cup ketchup
- ⅛   teaspoon pepper
- 8   slices (¾ oz each) American cheese or American cheese product
- 1   can (7.5 oz) refrigerated biscuits or refrigerated buttermilk biscuits

$1.33 *per serving*

1   Heat oven to 400°F. In 12-inch nonstick skillet, cook beef, onion and bell pepper over medium-high heat 5 to 7 minutes, stirring occasionally, until beef is thoroughly cooked; drain.

2   Stir in tomato sauce, ketchup and pepper; simmer 5 minutes, stirring occasionally. Into ungreased 2-quart casserole, spoon ⅓ of beef mixture. Top with 4 slices of the cheese. Repeat layers once. Top with remaining beef mixture, spreading to edge of casserole.

3   Separate dough into 10 biscuits. Arrange biscuits in single layer around edge of hot mixture in casserole.

4   Bake 13 to 17 minutes or until biscuits are golden brown.

1 Serving: Calories 420; Total Fat 22g (Saturated Fat 11g; Trans Fat 1g); Cholesterol 90mg; Sodium 1320mg; Total Carbohydrate 28g (Dietary Fiber 2g) **Exchanges:** 1½ Starch, ½ Other Carbohydrate, 3 Medium-Fat Meat, 1 Fat **Carbohydrate Choices:** 2

$mart $avings

American cheese melts easily, but slices of Cheddar or mozzarella cheese can be used. Watch for refrigerated biscuits on sale, and stock up. Be sure to store them in the coldest part of the refrigerator, and keep them cold until just before baking.

Mom's Skillet Goulash

Goulash is a well-known comfort food, and every family has their own favorite recipe. Here's an easy and inexpensive version that could become your new comfort goulash.

Prep Time: 30 Minutes | **Start to Finish:** 30 Minutes | 6 servings

8 oz uncooked rotini pasta (2 ²/₃ cups)

1 lb lean (at least 80%) ground beef

3 medium stalks celery, chopped (1¹/₂ cups)

1 large onion, chopped (1 cup)

2 cans (14.5 oz each) diced tomatoes, undrained

1 can (10³/₄ oz) condensed tomato soup

1 teaspoon dried basil leaves

¹/₂ teaspoon salt

¹/₄ teaspoon pepper

$1.32 *per serving*

1 Cook and drain pasta as directed on package.

2 Meanwhile, in 12-inch nonstick skillet or Dutch oven, cook beef, celery and onion over medium-high heat 5 to 7 minutes, stirring frequently, until beef is thoroughly cooked; drain.

3 Stir in cooked pasta and remaining ingredients. Heat to boiling. Reduce heat to low; simmer uncovered 10 minutes, stirring occasionally.

1 Serving: Calories 350; Total Fat 10g (Saturated Fat 3.5g; Trans Fat 0.5g); Cholesterol 45mg; Sodium 910mg; Total Carbohydrate 46g (Dietary Fiber 5g) **Exchanges:** 2 Starch, ¹/₂ Other Carbohydrate, 1 Vegetable, 2 Medium-Fat Meat **Carbohydrate Choices:** 3

$mart $avings

You can use other pasta shapes, such as elbow macaroni, rotelle, fusilli, penne or medium shells. Diced tomatoes come in several varieties, such as with roasted garlic, basil, garlic & oregano, or green chiles. Feel free to spice up your goulash by using diced tomatoes with added flavor.

Chili Mac 'n Cheese

This two-in-one skillet is sure to please everyone with its just-a-little-spicy kick.

Prep Time: 30 Minutes | **Start to Finish:** 30 Minutes | 6 servings

1 lb lean (at least 80%) ground beef

7 oz uncooked rotini pasta (2⅓ cups)

1 teaspoon chili powder

2¼ cups hot water

1 can (14.5 oz) diced tomatoes with zesty mild green chiles, undrained

2 cups shredded taco-flavored cheese (8 oz)

$1.20 *per serving*

1 In 12-inch skillet, cook beef over medium-high heat 5 to 7 minutes, stirring occasionally, until thoroughly cooked; drain.

2 Stir in uncooked pasta, chili powder, hot water and tomatoes. Heat to boiling, stirring frequently. Reduce heat to medium-low; cover and simmer 10 to 12 minutes, stirring occasionally, until pasta is tender.

3 Remove from heat; let stand uncovered 5 minutes. Stir in cheese until melted.

1 Serving: Calories 430; Total Fat 22g (Saturated Fat 11g; Trans Fat 1g); Cholesterol 85mg; Sodium 480mg; Total Carbohydrate 30g (Dietary Fiber 3g) **Exchanges:** 2 Starch, 3 Medium-Fat Meat, 1 Fat **Carbohydrate Choices:** 2

$mart $avings

If you prefer more heat, use diced tomatoes with jalapeño chiles instead. Check the refrigerator for some classic chili toppings to serve with this skillet meal—sour cream, guacamole, chopped green onion, sliced olives, chopped cilantro or sliced jalapeños.

Beef and Vegetable Noodle Dinner

Start with an inexpensive package of ramen noodle soup mix, and end up with a hearty ground beef skillet meal in only 20 minutes.

Prep Time: 20 Minutes | **Start to Finish:** 20 Minutes | 4 servings

1   lb extra-lean (at least 90%) ground beef

1   medium onion, chopped (½ cup)

1   can (14.5 oz) diced tomatoes with basil, garlic and oregano, undrained

1   cup water

1   teaspoon Italian seasoning

1   package (3 oz) beef-flavor ramen noodle soup mix

1½   cups frozen cut green beans

$**1.28** *per serving*

1   In 12-inch nonstick skillet, cook beef and onion over medium-high heat 5 to 7 minutes, stirring frequently, until beef is thoroughly cooked; drain.

2   Stir in tomatoes, water, Italian seasoning and contents of seasoning packet. Heat to boiling. Break up noodles; stir noodles and beans into beef mixture.

3   Heat to boiling. Reduce heat to low; cover and simmer about 5 minutes, stirring occasionally, until noodles and beans are tender.

1 Serving: Calories 320; Total Fat 14g (Saturated Fat 5g; Trans Fat 2g); Cholesterol 70mg; Sodium 550mg; Total Carbohydrate 23g (Dietary Fiber 4g) **Exchanges:** 1 Starch, 1 Vegetable, 3 Medium-Fat Meat **Carbohydrate Choices:** 1½

$mart $avings

Ramen noodle soup mix makes a quick and inexpensive lunch, so stock up when it's on sale. To break up the noodles before adding to the skillet, hit the unopened package a few times with a rolling pin or small saucepan. Or, break up the noodles with your hands after the package is open.

Ground Beef-and Corn-Topped Potato Skins

Who doesn't love a stuffed baked potato? This main-dish potato is not only economical but also easy using the microwave.

Prep Time: 25 Minutes | **Start to Finish:** 30 Minutes | 4 servings

2   large russet or Idaho baking potatoes (8 to 10 oz each)

½   lb lean (at least 80%) ground beef

½   teaspoon salt

¼   teaspoon pepper

1   cup frozen whole kernel corn

1   can (8 oz) tomato sauce

2   green onions, sliced (2 tablespoons)

1   small tomato, chopped

¼   cup sour cream

Chopped chives, if desired

$1.05 *per serving*

1 Pierce potatoes with fork; place on microwavable paper towel in microwave. Microwave on High 8 to 10 minutes, turning after 4 to 5 minutes, until tender. Let stand about 5 minutes or until cool enough to handle.

2 Meanwhile, in 10-inch skillet, cook beef, salt and pepper over medium-high heat 5 to 7 minutes, stirring frequently, until beef is thoroughly cooked; drain. Stir in corn, tomato sauce, onions and tomato. Cook 3 to 4 minutes, stirring occasionally, until hot and bubbly.

3 Cut potatoes in half lengthwise. Scoop out about 2 tablespoons of pulp from center of each half; place in medium bowl. Reserve potato shells. Mash potato pulp with fork. Stir in sour cream; set aside.

4 Spoon beef mixture into potato shells. Top each with about ¼ cup potato and sour cream mixture. Place on microwavable platter. Microwave uncovered on High 4 to 6 minutes or until hot. Sprinkle with chives. Serve immediately.

1 Serving: Calories 290; Total Fat 10g (Saturated Fat 4g; Trans Fat 0.5g); Cholesterol 45mg; Sodium 630mg; Total Carbohydrate 36g (Dietary Fiber 4g) **Exchanges:** 2 Starch, ½ Other Carbohydrate, 1 Medium-Fat Meat, ½ Fat **Carbohydrate Choices:** 2 ½

$mart $avings

If you have salsa on hand, use about 1 cup for the can of tomato sauce. And if your family likes peas, use 1 cup frozen instead of the corn for a change. A partial container of chive-and-onion sour cream potato topper in the fridge? Use ¼ cup instead of the sour cream.

Pizza Skillet
Hot Dish

All the wonderful flavors of pizza and the comfort of a "hot dish" without turning on the oven!

Prep Time: 30 Minutes | **Start to Finish:** 35 Minutes | 4 servings

½ lb lean (at least 80%) ground beef

2 oz sliced pepperoni, chopped (½ cup)

1 jar (14 oz) tomato pasta sauce

1 cup water

1 package (7 oz) ready-cut spaghetti (short curved spaghetti)

¼ cup sliced ripe olives

½ bell pepper (any color), cut into bite-size strips

1 cup shredded mozzarella cheese (4 oz)

$1.78 *per serving*

1 In 12-inch skillet, cook beef over medium-high heat 5 to 7 minutes, stirring frequently, until thoroughly cooked. Add pepperoni; cook 1 minute. Drain.

2 Stir in pasta sauce, water and uncooked spaghetti. Heat to boiling; stir. Reduce heat to medium-low; cover and cook 10 to 15 minutes, stirring occasionally, until spaghetti is of desired doneness.

3 Gently stir in olives. Arrange pepper strips over top. Sprinkle with cheese. Remove from heat. Cover; let stand 3 to 5 minutes or until cheese is melted.

1 Serving: Calories 600; Total Fat 24g (Saturated Fat 9g; Trans Fat 0.5g); Cholesterol 65mg; Sodium 1130mg; Total Carbohydrate 66g (Dietary Fiber 5g) **Exchanges:** 3 Starch, 1 ½ Other Carbohydrate, 3 Medium-Fat Meat, 1 Fat **Carbohydrate Choices:** 4 ½

$mart $avings

Hungry for pizza skillet hot dish but have no pepperoni? Use ½ pound Italian sausage for the pepperoni, or omit the pepperoni and use 1 pound ground beef. Cook the Italian sausage with the ground beef. For cheese lovers, sprinkle ¼ cup shredded Parmesan cheese over the pepper strips before sprinkling with the mozzarella cheese.

Cheeseburger Pizza

What do you do when the kids want cheeseburgers and the adults are hungry for pizza? No need to choose! Satisfy everyone with this homemade double-duty dinner.

Prep Time: 20 Minutes | **Start to Finish:** 40 Minutes | 8 servings

1   can (11 oz) refrigerated thin pizza crust

1   lb lean (at least 80%) ground beef

½   medium onion, thinly sliced (about ½ cup)

⅛   teaspoon pepper

⅓   cup pickle relish (not sweet)

¾   cup ketchup

1   tablespoon yellow mustard

4   slices bacon, crisply cooked, crumbled

1½   cups shredded American cheese (6 oz)

1   cup shredded lettuce

½   cup chopped tomato

$1.24 *per serving*

1   Heat oven to 400°F. Spray or grease 15×10×1-inch or larger dark or nonstick cookie sheet. Unroll dough on cookie sheet; starting at center, press dough into 15×10-inch rectangle.

2   In 10-inch nonstick skillet, cook beef, onion and pepper over medium-high heat 5 to 7 minutes, stirring occasionally, until thoroughly cooked; drain. Stir in relish, ketchup and mustard. Spoon evenly over dough. Sprinkle with bacon and cheese.

3   Bake 14 to 19 minutes or until crust is golden brown and cheese is melted. Top with lettuce and tomato. Serve immediately.

1 Serving: Calories 350; Total Fat 18g (Saturated Fat 8g; Trans Fat 0.5g); Cholesterol 60mg; Sodium 910mg; Total Carbohydrate 26g (Dietary Fiber 1g) **Exchanges:** 1 Starch, ½ Other Carbohydrate, 2 ½ Medium-Fat Meat, 1 Fat **Carbohydrate Choices:** 2

$mart $avings

When ground turkey is on sale, use it for the ground beef. It will save a few calories—and to save more, omit the bacon. If you don't have pickle relish, you may want to top the pizza with dill pickle sandwich slices before topping with lettuce and tomato.

Double-Meat Personal Pizzas

Four individual pizzas on one pan, and everyone can "personalize" one before popping the pan into the oven.

Prep Time: 10 Minutes | **Start to Finish:** 30 Minutes | 4 pizzas

¹/₂ lb lean (at least 80%) ground beef

1 can (13.8 oz) refrigerated classic pizza crust

¹/₂ cup pizza sauce

¹/₄ teaspoon dried oregano leaves, if desired

¹/₂ package (3.5-oz size) sliced pepperoni

2 tablespoons grated Parmesan cheese

1¹/₂ cups shredded Italian cheese blend (6 oz)

$2.08 *per serving*

1 Heat oven to 400°F. In 10-inch skillet, cook beef over medium-high heat 5 to 7 minutes, stirring frequently, until thoroughly cooked; drain.

2 Lightly spray large cookie sheet with cooking spray. Unroll dough on work surface. Cut dough into 4 equal pieces; place on cookie sheet. Press out each piece of dough to form 6×5-inch rectangle. With fingers, create slight rim on edge of each dough rectangle. Bake 8 minutes. Spread about 2 tablespoons pizza sauce just to rim of each crust; sprinkle with oregano. Top with pepperoni, beef and cheeses.

3 Bake 8 to 10 minutes or until cheese in center is melted.

1 Pizza: Calories 570; Total Fat 27g (Saturated Fat 13g; Trans Fat 1g); Cholesterol 80mg; Sodium 1510mg; Total Carbohydrate 51g (Dietary Fiber 0g) **Exchanges:** 3 Starch, ¹/₂ Other Carbohydrate, 3 High-Fat Meat **Carbohydrate Choices:** 3 ¹/₂

$mart $avings

Let the family check the fridge and pantry shelves for what they might like on their personal pizzas—maybe mozzarella or Cheddar cheese, those few olives in the jar, some chopped onion or a few slices of tomato—whatever will make their pizza special for them.

Cheeseburger Tacos

For the die-hard cheeseburger fan, add pickle slices to these cheeseburger tacos.

Prep Time: 20 Minutes | **Start to Finish:** 20 Minutes | 6 servings

1 box (4.6 oz) taco shells
   (12 shells)

12 slices (²/₃ oz each) American
   cheese

1 lb lean (at least 80%) ground beef

1 cup cheese 'n salsa dip

12 lettuce leaves

12 tomato slices

³/₄ cup chunky-style salsa

$2.04 *per serving*

1 Heat oven to 350°F. Line each taco shell with 1 slice of cheese. Arrange taco shells on ungreased cookie sheet (cheese will fall to one side). Bake 5 to 7 minutes or until cheese is melted.

2 Meanwhile, in 8-inch skillet, cook beef over medium-high heat 5 to 7 minutes, stirring frequently, until thoroughly cooked; drain. Stir in dip. Cook until hot.

3 To serve, spoon about 2 tablespoons beef mixture into each warm taco shell. Top each with lettuce and tomato. Serve with chunky-style salsa.

1 Serving (2 tacos each): Calories 220; Total Fat 15g (Saturated Fat 6g; Trans Fat 1g); Cholesterol 45mg; Sodium 650mg; Total Carbohydrate 12g (Dietary Fiber 1g) **Exchanges:** 1 Starch, 1 Medium-Fat Meat, 2 Fat **Carbohydrate Choices:** 1

$mart $avings

Leftover cheese 'n salsa dip? Spoon on hamburgers or hot dogs for an easy cheese topping. Or, toss with hot cooked pasta to make a quick "mac 'n cheese" for the kids' lunch. If you have a jar of processed cheese dip on hand, use 1 cup and add a 4-ounce can of chopped green chiles instead of buying the cheese 'n salsa dip.

Cheesy Hot Beef Sandwiches

Just 1 1/2 pounds of ground beef and a loaf of French bread make 8 hearty sandwiches to feed the family or serve for casual entertaining.

Prep Time: 20 Minutes | **Start to Finish:** 45 Minutes | 8 sandwiches

1 1/2 lb extra-lean (at least 90%) ground beef

1 package French onion soup mix (from 2.6-oz box)

1/4 cup water

1/2 medium bell pepper (any color), chopped (about 1/2 cup)

2 tablespoons chopped fresh parsley, if desired

2 cups shredded Cheddar–Monterey Jack cheese blend (8 oz)

1 loaf (1 lb) French bread, about 24 inches long

$**1.31** *per serving*

1 Heat oven to 350°F. Cut 26×18-inch piece of heavy-duty foil. In 12-inch nonstick skillet, cook beef over medium-high heat 5 to 7 minutes, stirring occasionally, until thoroughly cooked; drain. Add soup mix, water, bell pepper and parsley. Cook 2 to 3 minutes or until hot. Stir in cheese until melted.

2 Cut 1/2-inch lengthwise slice from top of French bread; set aside. With fork, remove inside of bread, leaving 1/2 inch around edges. Place loaf on foil. If desired, reserve bread pieces for another use. Fill indentation in bread with beef mixture. Place top of bread over beef. Wrap loaf in foil. Place on ungreased cookie sheet.

3 Bake 20 to 25 minutes or until hot. For sandwiches, cut loaf into 8 crosswise sections.

1 Sandwich: Calories 410; Total Fat 18g (Saturated Fat 9g; Trans Fat 1g); Cholesterol 80mg; Sodium 940mg; Total Carbohydrate 32g (Dietary Fiber 2g) **Exchanges:** 2 Starch, 3 Medium-Fat Meat, 1/2 Fat **Carbohydrate Choices:** 2

Preparing the Bread

Making the Sandwiches

$mart $avings

Make soft bread crumbs from the bread that was removed from the loaf by tearing it into small pieces. You could also toss the bread crumbs with some melted butter, and sprinkle on top of a casserole before baking. Or toast them in butter in a small skillet until golden brown. Then toss with some shredded Parmesan cheese and grated lemon peel, and sprinkle over drained cooked broccoli, asparagus or cauliflower.

Hoedown BBQ
Chuck Roast

Marinating this less expensive beef roast not only helps make it more tender, but also adds a nice Asian flavor. Serve the roast with new potatoes and sliced tomatoes.

Prep Time: 15 Minutes | **Start to Finish:** 7 Hours 45 Minutes | 8 servings

1   boneless beef chuck roast, 2 inches thick (4 lb)

¼   cup sugar

½   cup soy sauce

½   cup ketchup

¼   cup red wine vinegar

1   to 2 cloves garlic, finely chopped

⅛   teaspoon pepper

$**2.46** *per serving*

1   Trim fat from beef roast. In ungreased 12×8-inch (2-quart) glass baking dish, mix remaining ingredients. Add roast; turn to coat. Cover dish; refrigerate at least 6 hours but no longer than 24 hours, turning once or twice, to marinate.

2   Heat oven to 325°F. Place roast in shallow roasting pan; bake 1 hour 15 minutes to 1 hour 30 minutes, turning once. Baste with reserved marinade during last 15 minutes of bake time. Discard any remaining marinade.

1 Serving: Calories 460; Total Fat 27g (Saturated Fat 10g; Trans Fat 1g); Cholesterol 130mg; Sodium 1190mg; Total Carbohydrate 12g (Dietary Fiber 0g) **Exchanges:** 1 Other Carbohydrate, 6 Lean Meat, 1½ Fat **Carbohydrate Choices:** 1

Grilled Hoedown BBQ Chuck Roast: Heat gas or charcoal grill. Remove roast from marinade; reserve and refrigerate marinade until ready to use. Place roast on grill over medium-low heat. Cover grill; cook 50 to 65 minutes or until 160°F for medium doneness, turning once. Baste with reserved marinade during last 15 minutes of cook time. Discard any remaining marinade.

$mart $avings

Check what's on sale because you can use a 4-pound boneless chuck arm, shoulder or blade pot roast. Red wine vinegar adds a nice flavor, but apple cider or rice wine vinegar can also be used. Leftover pot roast is good shredded or chopped and used for taco, burrito or enchilada fillings, or heated with a jar of beef gravy for great hot beef sandwiches.

Chunky Beef
Chili

Beef stew meat, made from a less tender cut of beef, is less expensive than steak and makes a chunky chili that is just as filling and satisfying.

Prep Time: 15 Minutes | **Start to Finish:** 2 Hours 15 Minutes | 10 servings

- 1 tablespoon vegetable oil
- 2 lb beef stew meat, cut into ³/₄-inch cubes
- 4 medium cloves garlic, finely chopped
- 1 package (1 ³/₈ oz) chili seasoning mix
- 1 can (28 oz) crushed tomatoes, undrained
- 1 ³/₄ cups beef-flavored broth (from 32-oz carton)
- 1 can or bottle (12 oz) beer or ³/₄ cup beef-flavored broth
- 1 can (6 oz) tomato paste
- 2 cans (15 oz each) spicy chili beans in sauce, undrained
  Sour cream, if desired
  Shredded Cheddar cheese, if desired

$1.65 *per serving*

1 In 5-quart Dutch oven, heat oil over medium-high heat until hot. Add stew meat and garlic; cook, stirring occasionally, until beef is browned. Stir in chili seasoning mix. Stir in tomatoes, broth, beer and tomato paste. Heat to boiling. Reduce heat to low; cover and simmer 2 hours, stirring once halfway through cooking.

2 About 15 minutes before serving, stir in beans. Cook 10 to 15 minutes longer or until beans are hot. Top individual servings with sour cream and shredded cheese.

1 Serving (1 ¼ cups each): Calories 400; Total Fat 22g (Saturated Fat 10g; Trans Fat 0.5g); Cholesterol 80mg; Sodium 1270mg; Total Carbohydrate 24g (Dietary Fiber 6g) **Exchanges:** 1 Starch, ½ Other Carbohydrate, 3 ½ Lean Meat, 2 Fat **Carbohydrate Choices:** 1 ½

$mart $avings

If you have ground beef in the freezer or it's on sale, use 2 pounds for the stew meat. Reduce the simmer time to 1 hour to develop the flavors. To stretch this chili, add an extra can of beans, and serve with toppings such as shredded cheese, sour cream and some corn chips to add a little crunch.

Bow Ties with Bacon and Tomatoes

A few slices of smoky bacon add lots of flavor without adding lots of expense to this pasta skillet dinner.

Prep Time: 30 Minutes | **Start to Finish:** 30 Minutes | 4 servings

4	slices bacon, cut into 1-inch pieces
1	medium onion, finely chopped (½ cup)
1	can (14.5 oz) diced tomatoes with roasted garlic and onion, undrained
1 ³/₄	cups chicken broth (from 32-oz carton)
6	oz uncooked bow tie (farfalle) pasta (3 cups)
¹/₈	teaspoon pepper

$0.86 *per serving*

1 In 12-inch skillet, cook bacon over medium-high heat 8 to 10 minutes, stirring frequently, until bacon is crisp; drain if necessary. Reduce heat to medium. Add onion; cook 2 to 3 minutes, stirring frequently, until onion is tender. Drain if necessary.

2 Stir in tomatoes, broth, uncooked pasta and pepper. Heat to boiling over high heat. Reduce heat to medium; cook uncovered 10 to 12 minutes, stirring occasionally, until pasta is tender and mixture thickens to the desired consistency.

1 Serving: Calories 440; Total Fat 11g (Saturated Fat 3.5g; Trans Fat 0g); Cholesterol 15mg; Sodium 990mg; Total Carbohydrate 66g (Dietary Fiber 5g) **Exchanges:** 4 Starch, 1 ½ Vegetable, ½ High-Fat Meat, 1 Fat **Carbohydrate Choices:** 4 ½

$mart $avings

Have a few hot dogs in the fridge or a piece of kielbasa or Polish sausage? Cut into thin slices and sauté in a tablespoon of vegetable oil instead of using bacon.

Sour Cream Beef Skillet Supper

This is an easy twist on classic stroganoff because the noodles are cooked with the beef and sour cream—plus peas are added to create a one-dish meal.

Prep Time: 20 Minutes | **Start to Finish:** 20 Minutes | 4 servings

1   medium onion, sliced ($\frac{1}{2}$ cup)

1   cup water

1$\frac{3}{4}$ cups beef-flavored broth (from 32-oz carton)

8   oz uncooked wide egg noodles (4$\frac{1}{2}$ cups)

1   cup frozen sweet peas

1   teaspoon paprika

$\frac{1}{2}$ lb cooked roast beef, cut into thin bite-size strips

1   cup sour cream

2   medium green onions, sliced (2 tablespoons), if desired

$2.02 *per serving*

1 Spray 12-inch skillet or 5-quart Dutch oven with cooking spray; heat over medium-high heat. Add onion; cook and stir 2 to 3 minutes or until crisp-tender.

2 Stir in water, broth, uncooked noodles, frozen peas and paprika. Heat to boiling. Reduce heat to medium-low; cover and simmer 6 to 8 minutes, stirring occasionally, until noodles are desired doneness and liquid is almost absorbed.

3 Stir in beef and sour cream. Cook 1 to 2 minutes longer, stirring constantly, just until hot. Sprinkle with green onions.

1 Serving: Calories 500; Total Fat 23g (Saturated Fat 11g; Trans Fat 1g); Cholesterol 125mg; Sodium 520mg; Total Carbohydrate 47g (Dietary Fiber 3g) **Exchanges:** 2 Starch, $\frac{1}{2}$ Other Carbohydrate, 1 Vegetable, 2$\frac{1}{2}$ Lean Meat, 3 Fat **Carbohydrate Choices:** 3

$mart $avings

This is a great way to use leftover cooked beef roast or steak. You will need about 2 cups beef strips or cubes. Watch for deli roast beef on sale, and order $\frac{1}{2}$ pound, sliced about $\frac{1}{2}$ inch thick, so it's easy to cut into bite-sized strips. Peas go nicely with beef and sour cream, but other frozen vegetables, such as corn or broccoli, would also be good.

Bruschetta-Style Tortellini Salad

The flavors of an antipasto platter, including cheese, olives and pepperoni, are in this pasta salad, and the bruschetta dressing adds a nice fresh taste. Toasted French bread slices are a nice accompaniment to the salad.

Prep Time: 20 Minutes | **Start to Finish:** 1 Hour 20 Minutes | 6 servings

Bruschetta Dressing

1 **can (14.5 oz) diced tomatoes, drained, juice reserved**

¼ **cup chopped fresh basil leaves**

2 **tablespoons olive oil**

1 **clove garlic, finely chopped**

Salad

1 **package (20 oz) refrigerated cheese-filled tortellini**

2 **cups sliced fresh mushrooms (about 5 oz)**

1 **cup cubed mozzarella cheese**

½ **medium red onion, chopped (½ cup)**

1 **can (2 ¼ oz) sliced ripe olives, drained**

½ **package (3.5-oz size) sliced pepperoni, cut in half**

$**2.30** *per serving*

1   In medium bowl, mix dressing ingredients.

2   Cook and drain tortellini as directed on package. Rinse with cold water to cool; drain. In large bowl, toss tortellini with dressing, mushrooms, cheese, onion, olives and pepperoni; stir in reserved tomato juice.

3   Cover and refrigerate at least 1 hour but no longer than 4 hours before serving.

1 Serving: Calories 280; Total Fat 11g (Saturated Fat 4.5g; Trans Fat 0g); Cholesterol 35mg; Sodium 510mg; Total Carbohydrate 31g (Dietary Fiber 2g) **Exchanges:** 2 Starch, 1 High-Fat Meat, ½ Fat **Carbohydrate Choices:** 2

$mart $avings

Watch for a container (16 ounces) of fresh bruschetta mix on sale, and use it instead of making the dressing. If you have other olives, slice them and use instead of the ripe olives.

Tuna Divan Crescent Squares

No need to serve bread with this twist on the classic turkey and broccoli divan. Crescent rolls form the crust to make this a hearty meal-in-a dish.

Prep Time: 20 Minutes | **Start to Finish:** 55 Minutes | 8 servings

1   can (8 oz) refrigerated crescent dinner rolls

1   cup shredded Swiss cheese (4 oz)

1   box (9 oz) frozen broccoli cuts, cooked, well drained

4   eggs

1   can (10 ¾ oz) condensed cream of broccoli soup

2   tablespoons mayonnaise or salad dressing

½   teaspoon onion powder

½   teaspoon dried dill weed

1   can (5 or 6 oz) tuna in water, drained

1   jar (2 oz) diced pimientos, drained

$**1.37** *per serving*

1   Heat oven to 350°F. Unroll dough on work surface, and separate into 2 long rectangles; place lengthwise in ungreased 13×9-inch pan. Press in bottom and ½ inch up sides of pan to form crust; press edges and perforations to seal. Sprinkle cheese over crust; arrange broccoli over cheese.

2   In medium bowl, beat eggs slightly with whisk. Beat in soup, mayonnaise, onion powder and dill weed. Stir in tuna and pimientos. Pour evenly over broccoli.

3   Bake 28 to 32 minutes or until filling is set. Cut into squares.

1 Serving: Calories 280; Total Fat 17g (Saturated Fat 6g; Trans Fat 1.5g); Cholesterol 125mg; Sodium 600mg; Total Carbohydrate 17g (Dietary Fiber 1g) **Exchanges:** 1 Starch, 1 ½ Medium-Fat Meat, 2 Fat **Carbohydrate Choices:** 1

Chicken Divan Crescent Squares: Substitute 1 can (5 or 6 oz) chicken, drained, for the tuna and 1 can (10 ¾ oz) cream of chicken soup for the broccoli soup.

$mart $avings

Pimientos add a nice touch of color, but you can omit them or use ¼ cup chopped bell pepper if you have some on hand. Also, the small pimiento jar is great for storing bulk spices or herbs, which can be purchased in small amounts. Cream of broccoli soup enhances the broccoli flavor, but use any cream soup you have in the pantry.

Italian Bean and Tuna Salad

Beans are inexpensive, and this Italian bean and tuna salad is a tasty way to include beans in your weekly menu.

Prep Time: 20 Minutes | **Start to Finish:** 2 Hours 20 Minutes | 4 servings

1 **can (15 or 19 oz) cannellini beans, drained, rinsed**

1 **can (5 oz) white tuna in water, drained, flaked**

1 **cup fresh green beans, trimmed, cut into 1-inch pieces, cooked, and rinsed with cold water**

2 **medium stalks celery, chopped (1 cup)**

1 **small bell pepper (any color), chopped (½ cup)**

3 **tablespoons chopped fresh chives**

2 **tablespoons chopped fresh parsley**

½ **cup reduced-calorie or fat-free Italian dressing**

½ **teaspoon dried oregano leaves**

   Lettuce leaves, if desired

1 In medium bowl, mix all ingredients except lettuce. Cover and refrigerate at least 2 hours to blend flavors.

2 Just before serving, place lettuce in serving bowl or on individual plates; spoon salad onto lettuce.

1 Serving: Calories 270; Total Fat 6g (Saturated Fat 1g; Trans Fat 0g); Cholesterol 10mg; Sodium 530mg; Total Carbohydrate 33g (Dietary Fiber 8g) **Exchanges:** 1 Starch, 1 Other Carbohydrate, 1 Vegetable, 2 Lean Meat **Carbohydrate Choices:** 2

$mart $avings

Usually white beans are used for this salad, but you can use a 16- to 19-ounce can of navy, kidney, black or lima beans, drained and rinsed, for the cannellini beans. If fresh green beans aren't at their peak, use 1 cup frozen green beans, cooked and rinsed with cold water. The fresh chives and parsley add a nice fresh flavor, but if you don't have them available, omit them or add ¼ cup chopped green onions.

$1.85 *per serving*

CHAPTER 2

Saved by the Slow Cooker

If only taking it slow was always an option. Even when you can't, your slow cooker can. Slow and low, as in low prep, low cleanup and low cost. And you get a home filled with the unmistakable scent of all-day simmering and flavors mingling to remind you that slow is good—and dinner is ready.

Ode to a Slow Cooker

There are so many reasons to love thee, trusty countertop appliance. Chief among them: The savings. Oh, the savings! Let us count the ways.

SAVINGS #1

Money Slow cookers allow you to cook cheaper cuts of meat. Period. It's exactly what they're designed to do. See, the most-exercised parts of an animal—the leg and shoulder, for example—yield the toughest meat. These cuts are often passed over in favor of more tender quick to cook pieces. But the very process of using a slow cooker tenderizes, making low-cost meat taste high-dollar delicious. It's not all about meat, though. Slow cookers are fantastic for cooking budget-friendly legumes, such as beans and dried peas, too.

SAVINGS #2

Headache Talk about low-maintenance. Just (a) toss ingredients into one crock, then (b) turn it on. Slow cookers do their work best if you forget about them for hours. Literally. It's not neglect. It's home cooking at its simplest.

SAVINGS #3

Time Most recipes involve minimal prep time up front, and cooking is as simple as flipping a switch. Once the slow cooker's done its thing, there's just one crock to clean, and slow cooker liners can even cut that out of the equation. Plan well, and what you've made is more than one dinner—it's the quick-start base for time-saving meals throughout the week.

Meet Your Match

All slow cookers are not created equal. Consider your family's specific preferences and needs when choosing this budget-cooking essential.

Crock Most are removable, but check to make sure. You'll appreciate the easy prep and cleaning. Some are even dishwasher safe.

Size & Shape Typical slow cookers range from three to seven quarts, either round or oval, which can accommodate a roast. Bigger is not automatically better. It should be at least half full to work properly, and you'll need to be able to store it. Consider your family size, entertaining needs and storage space.

Extras These days, slow cookers come with all sorts of perks—programmable start, temperature control, the ability to automatically switch to "warm" after cooking. Others have a simple dial with two settings: High and Low. Of course bells and whistles add cost. Decide what you can and can't live without.

Don't Lift the Lid!

Sure, it's tempting to get a first-hand look at what's generating such a fantastic smell. But condensation on the glass lid has formed a nice water seal, which helps lock in flavor and heat. Break that seal, and the temperature drops 10 to 15 degrees, meaning your dish will now require 20 to 30 extra minutes of cook time. Resist temptation and let your slow cooker do its thing.

Turkey Breast with Vegetables

Turkey isn't just for Thanksgiving. Turkey is a good price value—enjoy this easy slow-simmered turkey dinner any time of the year.

Prep Time: 20 Minutes | **Start to Finish:** 7 Hours 20 Minutes | 10 servings

3 medium red potatoes, cut into 1-inch pieces (about 4 cups)

8 medium carrots, cut into 1-inch pieces (about 2 cups)

1 small onion, cut into wedges (½ cup)

1 bone-in turkey breast with gravy packet (5 to 6 lb)

$1.66 *per serving*

1 In 5- to 6-quart slow cooker, mix potatoes, carrots, onion and gravy from turkey breast. Place turkey breast on top.

2 Cover; cook on Low heat setting 7 to 8 hours or until vegetables are tender and meat thermometer inserted in center of turkey reads 170°F.

1 Serving: Calories 380; Total Fat 15g (Saturated Fat 4g; Trans Fat 0g); Cholesterol 120mg; Sodium 400mg; Total Carbohydrate 16g (Dietary Fiber 2g) **Exchanges:** 1 Starch, 6 Lean Meat **Carbohydrate Choices:** 1

$mart $avings

Freeze any leftover turkey to use later in recipes calling for cooked turkey or chicken. Just chop, slice or shred, put it in an airtight container with a lid, label it with the name of the recipe you plan to use it in, and freeze up to 4 months.

Tuscan Turkey and Beans

Inexpensive dried beans and thrifty turkey thighs are the perfect pairing for a slow-simmered dish in the slow cooker.

Prep Time: 30 Minutes | **Start to Finish:** 7 Hours 30 Minutes | 6 servings

6	cups water
16	oz dried navy beans (2 cups), sorted, rinsed
3	cups chicken broth (from 32-oz carton)
¼	cup olive oil
¾	cup chopped parsley
1	tablespoon Italian seasoning
12	medium cloves garlic, chopped (2 tablespoons)
1½	teaspoons salt
½	teaspoon pepper
1	package (1½ to 2¼ lb) turkey thighs, skin removed
1½	cups frozen cut green beans, thawed

$1.89 *per serving*

1 Spray 5-quart slow cooker with cooking spray. In 3-quart saucepan, heat water to boiling over medium-high heat. Add navy beans. Reduce heat to medium-low; simmer uncovered 10 minutes. Drain; rinse with cold water. Place beans in slow cooker; add broth.

2 Meanwhile, in medium bowl, stir together olive oil, ½ cup of the parsley, the Italian seasoning, garlic, ½ teaspoon of the salt and the pepper. Press mixture firmly onto turkey thighs. Place turkey on top of beans in slow cooker. Cover; cook on Low heat setting 7 to 9 hours.

3 Remove turkey from slow cooker. Increase heat setting to High. Stir green beans and remaining 1 teaspoon salt into slow cooker. Cover; cook 15 to 20 minutes or until vegetables are hot. Meanwhile, remove turkey from bones. To serve, place bean mixture in shallow bowls; top with turkey, and sprinkle with remaining ¼ cup parsley.

1 Serving: Calories 480; Total Fat 14g (Saturated Fat 2.5g; Trans Fat 0g); Cholesterol 90mg; Sodium 1080mg; Total Carbohydrate 49g (Dietary Fiber 19g) **Exchanges:** 2½ Starch, 2 Vegetable, 4 Lean Meat **Carbohydrate Choices:** 3

$mart $avings

This recipe would work equally well with pork or beef, so use a budget-friendly cut, such as pork shoulder or beef chuck roast. Try other types of dried beans you may have in your pantry, such as great northern, pinto or kidney beans.

Chicken Pot Roast Dinner

This is a more economical version of "pot roast" because it's made with chicken thighs rather than a beef roast.

Prep Time: 10 Minutes | **Start to Finish:** 8 Hours 25 Minutes | 6 servings

1 lb small potatoes (6 to 8), unpeeled, cut into 1-inch pieces (3 cups)

2 cups ready-to-eat baby-cut carrots

1 cup frozen small whole onions (from 1-lb bag), thawed

6 boneless skinless chicken thighs (1 ¼ lb)

½ teaspoon salt

⅛ teaspoon pepper

1 jar (12 oz) chicken gravy

1 ½ cups frozen sweet peas, thawed

$1.05 *per serving*

1 Spray 3- to 4-quart slow cooker with cooking spray. In cooker, place potatoes, carrots and onions. Sprinkle chicken with salt and pepper; place over vegetables in cooker. Pour gravy over top.

2 Cover; cook on Low heat setting 8 to 10 hours.

3 Stir in peas. Increase heat setting to High. Cover; cook about 15 minutes longer or until peas are tender.

1 Serving (1 ½ cups): Calories 310; Total Fat 11g (Saturated Fat 3g; Trans Fat 0g); Cholesterol 60mg; Sodium 630mg; Total Carbohydrate 28g (Dietary Fiber 4g) **Exchanges:** 1 ½ Starch, 1 ½ Vegetable, 2 ½ Lean Meat, ½ Fat **Carbohydrate Choices:** 2

$mart $avings

Chicken thighs are a good choice for the slow cooker because they're economical and stay moist and tender during the long slow cooking. If you have regular carrots rather than baby carrots, use 2 medium carrots, cut into 1-inch pieces.

Chicken
Tortilla Soup

This tortilla soup is packed with good things—chicken, corn and beans—to make a hearty soup that will satisfy both the appetite and the budget. Serve with tortilla chips on the side.

Prep Time: 10 Minutes | **Start to Finish:** 5 Hours 10 Minutes | 6 servings

6 boneless skinless chicken thighs (1 1/4 lb)

1 medium onion, chopped (1/2 cup)

3 corn tortillas (6 inch), cut into 1-inch pieces

1 1/2 cups frozen whole kernel corn, thawed

1 can (15 oz) chick peas or garbanzo beans, drained, rinsed

1 can (4.5 oz) chopped green chiles

3/4 cup salsa verde

1 carton (32 oz) chicken broth (4 cups)

1 teaspoon dried oregano leaves

1 teaspoon ground cumin

1/2 teaspoon ground red pepper (cayenne)

2 tomatoes, seeded, chopped

Chopped fresh cilantro leaves, if desired

$2.03 *per serving*

1 In 3- to 4-quart slow cooker, mix all ingredients except tomatoes and cilantro.

2 Cover; cook on Low heat setting 5 to 7 hours. Stir to break up chicken thighs. Stir in tomatoes before serving. Garnish with cilantro.

1 Serving (1 1/2 cups): Calories 390; Total Fat 11g (Saturated Fat 3g; Trans Fat 0g); Cholesterol 60mg; Sodium 1300mg; Total Carbohydrate 39g (Dietary Fiber 8g) **Exchanges:** 2 Starch, 1/2 Other Carbohydrate, 3 1/2 Lean Meat **Carbohydrate Choices:** 2 1/2

$mart $avings

Salsa verde is "green salsa," which is made from tomatillos, green chiles and cilantro. If you have "red" salsa, go ahead and use 3/4 cup for the salsa verde. Be sure to use corn tortillas—not flour tortillas—because the corn tortilla pieces will dissolve during cooking, adding flavor and some thickening to the soup.

Chicken and Rice Casserole

This chicken and rice dish is not only super easy to make but uses only five ingredients, so it is also super easy on the food budget.

Prep Time: 20 Minutes | **Start to Finish:** 5 Hours 5 Minutes | 4 servings

5 boneless skinless chicken thighs (about 1 lb), each cut into 4 pieces

1 can (10 ³/₄ oz) condensed cream of chicken soup

1 jar (4.5 oz) sliced mushrooms, undrained

¹/₂ cup water

1¹/₂ cups frozen sweet peas, thawed

1¹/₂ cups uncooked instant white rice

Salt and pepper, if desired

$1.59 *per serving*

1 Spray 3- to 4-quart slow cooker with cooking spray. In cooker, place chicken. Top with soup, mushrooms and water; stir gently to mix, and spread evenly over chicken.

2 Cover; cook on Low heat setting 4 hours 30 minutes to 5 hours 30 minutes.

3 About 15 minutes before serving, stir peas and rice into chicken mixture. Cover; cook on Low heat setting 10 to 15 minutes longer or until rice is tender. If desired, add salt and pepper.

1 Serving (1 ¹/₄ cups): Calories 460; Total Fat 15g (Saturated Fat 4.5g; Trans Fat 0g); Cholesterol 75mg; Sodium 780mg; Total Carbohydrate 50g (Dietary Fiber 3g) **Exchanges:** 2 Starch, 1 Other Carbohydrate, 1 Vegetable, 3 ¹/₂ Lean Meat, ¹/₂ Fat **Carbohydrate Choices:** 3

$mart $avings

The cream of chicken soup enhances the chicken flavor, but you can use cream of mushroom soup if it's on your pantry shelf. Have some leftover chicken broth in the refrigerator? Use it in place of the water if you like.

Spaghetti with Slow-Simmered Meat Sauce

Spaghetti sauce simmers long and slow in the slow cooker, so the flavors develop and meld together. And there's no tomato sauce splatter on the stovetop to clean up!

Prep Time: 45 Minutes | **Start to Finish:** 8 Hours 15 Minutes | 8 servings

1	lb lean (at least 80%) ground beef
1/2	lb bulk Italian pork sausage
1	medium onion, chopped (1/2 cup)
1	medium bell pepper (any color), chopped (1 cup)
2	cloves garlic, finely chopped
2	medium carrots, finely chopped (1 cup)
1	can (28 oz) crushed tomatoes, undrained
1	can (8 oz) tomato sauce
1	can (6 oz) tomato paste
1	tablespoon packed brown sugar
3	teaspoons Italian seasoning
1/2	teaspoon salt
1/4	teaspoon pepper
16	oz uncooked spaghetti
	Shredded Parmesan cheese, if desired

$1.40 *per serving*

1 In 12-inch skillet, cook beef and sausage over medium heat 8 to 10 minutes, stirring frequently, until beef is thoroughly cooked and sausage is no longer pink; drain.

2 Spray 3 1/2- to 4-quart slow cooker with cooking spray. In cooker, mix beef mixture and all remaining ingredients except spaghetti and Parmesan cheese.

3 Cover; cook on Low heat setting 8 to 10 hours.

4 About 20 minutes before serving, cook spaghetti as directed on package; drain. Serve sauce over cooked spaghetti. Sprinkle with Parmesan cheese.

1 Serving: Calories 460; Total Fat 12g (Saturated Fat 4g; Trans Fat 0g); Cholesterol 45mg; Sodium 750mg; Total Carbohydrate 64g (Dietary Fiber 6g) **Exchanges:** 3 Starch, 1 Other Carbohydrate, 1 Vegetable, 2 Medium-Fat Meat **Carbohydrate Choices:** 4

$mart $avings

Not serving eight for dinner tonight? Cook only as much spaghetti as you need, and serve it with just the right amount of sauce. Refrigerate or freeze the remaining sauce for another time.

Pot Roast with Creamy Dill Sauce

The creamy dill sauce adds a burst of flavor—without adding a burst of expense—to the popular beef pot roast. Cooking the pot roast in the slow cooker means you get less shrinkage and even more bang for your buck.

Prep Time: 30 Minutes | **Start to Finish:** 9 Hours 30 Minutes | 8 servings

Pot Roast

- 2 tablespoons all-purpose flour
- 1 teaspoon salt
- 1/2 teaspoon pepper
- 1 boneless chuck or bottom round beef pot roast (about 2 lb), trimmed of fat
- 1 cup beef broth (from 14-oz can or 32-oz carton)
- 1 tablespoon Dijon mustard
- 4 cloves garlic, finely chopped
- 1/2 teaspoon dried dill weed
- 1 large onion, cut into 12 wedges
- 1 bag (16 oz) ready-to-eat baby-cut carrots (about 30 carrots)
- 4 medium Yukon gold potatoes (about 1 1/4 lb), unpeeled, cut into 1-inch cubes

Sauce

- 2 tablespoons all-purpose flour
- 2 tablespoons water
- 1 teaspoon dried dill weed
- 1 cup fat-free sour cream

$2.03 *per serving*

1 In shallow bowl, mix 2 tablespoons flour, 1 teaspoon salt and the pepper. Place beef on flour mixture; turn to coat evenly.

2 Spray 5- to 6-quart slow cooker with cooking spray. Heat 12-inch nonstick skillet over medium-high heat. Add beef to skillet; cook about 5 minutes, turning once, until golden brown on both sides. Place in cooker.

3 In small bowl, mix broth, mustard, garlic and 1/2 teaspoon dill weed. Pour over beef in cooker. Place onion, carrots and potatoes on top of beef. (Place ingredients in that order so everything cooks evenly.)

4 Cover; cook on Low heat setting 9 to 10 hours.

5 Remove beef and vegetables from cooker; place on large cutting board; cover to keep warm. In small bowl, beat sauce ingredients except sour cream with whisk until smooth.

6 Strain any fat from liquid in cooker. Pour liquid into 1-quart saucepan; heat to boiling over high heat. Stir sauce mixture into hot liquid; cook 2 to 3 minutes, stirring constantly, until thickened. Remove from heat; stir in sour cream.

7 Cut beef into serving pieces. Serve sauce over beef and vegetables.

1 Serving: Calories 320; Total Fat 12g (Saturated Fat 4.5g; Trans Fat 0.5g); Cholesterol 60mg; Sodium 610mg; Total Carbohydrate 28g (Dietary Fiber 4g) **Exchanges:** 1 Starch, 1/2 Other Carbohydrate, 1 Vegetable, 2 1/2 Lean Meat, 1 Fat **Carbohydrate Choices:** 2

$mart $avings

Often the grain (muscles) changes direction in less tender cuts of meat, so it isn't always easy to get tender slices. To slice pot roast, place the roast on a cutting board. Hold the meat in place with a meat fork, and cut between the muscles. Remove one section of the meat at a time. Turn the section so that the grain of the meat runs parallel to the cutting board, and cut meat across the grain into slices.

French Dip Sandwiches

A less tender cut of meat? The slow cooker makes a popular hearty sandwich a deal that can't be beat.

Prep Time: 15 Minutes | **Start to Finish:** 8 Hours 15 Minutes | 12 sandwiches

1 large sweet onion, sliced

1 can (14 oz) beef broth (1 ¾ cup)

1 boneless beef rump roast (4 lb), trimmed of fat

2 tablespoons balsamic vinegar

1 package (0.7 oz) Italian dressing mix

½ teaspoon salt

¼ teaspoon freshly ground black pepper

12 hoagie buns, split

1 large green bell pepper, cut into strips

12 slices (1 oz each) provolone cheese, cut in halves

$**1.75** *per serving*

1 Spray 3- to 4-quart slow cooker with cooking spray. In cooker, place onion; add broth. Brush all surfaces of beef roast with vinegar. Place in cooker. Sprinkle with dressing mix, salt and pepper.

2 Cover; cook on Low heat setting 8 to 10 hours.

3 Remove beef from cooker; place on cutting board. Cut beef across grain into thin slices. Return slices to cooker; mix well.

4 With slotted spoon, place beef onto bottoms halves of buns. Top each with bell pepper, cheese and top half of bun. Ladle the juices from the cooker into small bowls; serve with the sandwiches for dipping.

1 Sandwich: Calories 550; Total Fat 16g (Saturated Fat 7g; Trans Fat 1g); Cholesterol 100mg; Sodium 1180mg; Total Carbohydrate 51g (Dietary Fiber 2g) **Exchanges:** 3 Starch, ½ Other Carbohydrate, 5 ½ Very Lean Meat, 2 Fat **Carbohydrate Choices:** 3 ½

$mart $avings

Don't need 12 sandwiches? Cover and refrigerate or freeze the remaining beef mixture for another time. Heat the beef mixture, thawed if frozen, in the microwave.

Chunky Beef and Vegetable Chili

This hearty chunky chili is great for "family chili night" or entertaining. Set out bowls of shredded cheese, chopped onion, chopped cilantro and sour cream so everyone can top their chili as they like.

Prep Time: 20 Minutes | **Start to Finish:** 9 Hours 50 Minutes | 7 servings

1 boneless beef chuck pot roast (about 1 1/2 lb), trimmed of fat, cut into 1/2-inch cubes

1 lb small red potatoes (about 9), unpeeled, quartered

2 medium carrots, sliced (1 cup)

1 large bell pepper (any color), coarsely chopped (about 1 1/2 cups)

1 large onion, chopped (1 cup)

2 large cloves garlic, finely chopped

1 can (15 oz) dark red kidney beans, drained, rinsed

1/2 teaspoon salt

1 carton (32 oz) beef broth (4 cups)

1 chipotle chile in adobo sauce, finely chopped (from 7-oz can)

1 tablespoon adobo sauce from can of chipotle chiles

3 tablespoons packed brown sugar

Sour cream, if desired

Shredded Cheddar cheese, if desired

$1.86 *per serving*

1 Spray 4- to 5-quart slow cooker with cooking spray. In cooker, mix all ingredients except chile, adobo sauce, brown sugar, sour cream and cheese.

2 Cover; cook on Low heat setting 9 to 10 hours.

3 Stir in chile, adobo sauce and brown sugar. Cover; cook 30 minutes longer. Stir well before serving. Top individual servings with sour cream and shredded cheese.

1 Serving (1 1/2 cups): Calories 350; Total Fat 11g (Saturated Fat 4g; Trans Fat 0g); Cholesterol 50mg; Sodium 1010mg; Total Carbohydrate 37g (Dietary Fiber 7g) **Exchanges:** 2 Starch, 1 Vegetable, 2 1/2 Lean Meat, 1/2 Fat **Carbohydrate Choices:** 2 1/2

$mart $avings

If you don't have chipotle chile in adobo sauce, use 1 tablespoon chili powder instead. You can easily stretch this chili by serving 1 cup over hot pasta, a piece of warm cornbread (split open) or a baked potato. Sprinkle with some shredded cheese and chopped green onion.

Smothered
Swiss Steak

Serve mashed potatoes and a crisp green salad with this steak-and-gravy dinner for a comfort meal that will make the family happy and content.

Prep Time: 15 Minutes | **Start to Finish:** 8 Hours 15 Minutes | 4 servings

2	teaspoons vegetable oil
1 ½	lb boneless beef top round steak (½ to ¾ inch thick), trimmed of fat
1	teaspoon salt
¼	teaspoon pepper
1	medium onion, halved lengthwise, thinly sliced
1	medium carrot, shredded (about ⅓ cup)
1	can (4 oz) mushroom pieces and stems, drained
1	can (10 ¾ oz) condensed cream of mushroom soup
1	can (8 oz) tomato sauce

$3.09 *per serving*

1 In 10-inch skillet, heat oil over medium-high heat. Cut beef into 4 equal pieces. Sprinkle beef with salt and pepper; place in skillet. Cook 4 to 6 minutes, turning once, until well browned.

2 Spray 3- to 4-quart slow cooker with cooking spray. In cooker, mix onion, carrot and mushrooms. Place beef in cooker over vegetables. In same skillet, mix soup and tomato sauce. Pour over beef.

3 Cover; cook on Low heat setting 8 to 10 hours. Stir sauce well before serving over beef.

1 Serving: Calories 330; Total Fat 12g (Saturated Fat 3.5g; Trans Fat 0g); Cholesterol 95mg; Sodium 1590mg; Total Carbohydrate 14g (Dietary Fiber 2g) **Exchanges:** ½ Other Carbohydrate, 1 Vegetable, 5 Lean Meat **Carbohydrate Choices:** 1

$mart $avings

If you have fresh mushrooms in the refrigerator, use about 1 cup sliced mushrooms for the canned ones. Found a small zucchini and a stalk of celery, too? Shred the zucchini, slice the celery and add them with the other vegetables. This is a great way to use up those extra veggies.

French Onion
Beef Steak

You can turn inexpensive, less tender cuts of steak into the wonderful flavors of classic French onion soup with lots of onions, tasty herb stuffing and gooey melted cheese. Serve with steamed baby carrots on the side.

Prep Time: 20 Minutes | **Start to Finish:** 8 Hours 30 Minutes | 6 servings

1¼ lb boneless beef round steak (½ to ¾ inch thick), trimmed of fat

1 package (8 oz) fresh mushrooms, sliced (3 cups)

1 large onion, sliced, separated into rings

1 can (10¾ oz) condensed French onion soup

1 package (6 oz) 10-minute herb stuffing mix

¼ cup butter or margarine, melted

1 cup shredded mozzarella cheese (4 oz)

$2.28 *per serving*

1 Spray 3½- to 4-quart slow cooker with cooking spray. Cut beef into 6 serving-size pieces. In cooker, layer half each of beef, mushrooms and onion; repeat layers. Pour soup over ingredients in slow cooker.

2 Cover; cook on Low heat setting 8 to 10 hours or until beef is tender and of desired doneness.

3 Before serving, in medium bowl, place stuffing mix, melted butter and ½ cup liquid from slow cooker; toss to mix. Place stuffing on top of contents in slow cooker.

4 Increase heat setting to High. Cover; cook about 10 minutes longer or until stuffing is fluffy. Sprinkle with cheese. Cover; cook until cheese is melted.

1 Serving: Calories 400; Total Fat 17g (Saturated Fat 9g; Trans Fat 0.5g); Cholesterol 85mg; Sodium 970mg; Total Carbohydrate 30g (Dietary Fiber 3g) **Exchanges:** 1 Starch, ½ Other Carbohydrate, 1 Vegetable, 4 Lean Meat, 1 Fat **Carbohydrate Choices:** 2

$mart $avings

Try other shredded cheese you may have on hand, such as provolone or Swiss cheese, in place of the mozzarella cheese. If you don't have a can of French onion soup, use beef broth instead. The onion flavor won't be as strong, but it will still taste delicious.

Round Steak
Stroganoff

Freeze half of the stroganoff for another meal. Thaw and heat it in the microwave. Serve it over pasta or over baked, mashed or fried potatoes, and baby carrots.

Prep Time: 15 Minutes | **Start to Finish:** 7 Hours 15 Minutes | 7 servings

1 ½ lb boneless beef round steak (½ to ¾ inch thick), trimmed of fat, cut into bite-size strips

2 tablespoons onion soup mix (from 1-oz package)

1 jar (4.5 oz) sliced mushrooms, drained

1 can (10 ¾ oz) condensed cream of mushroom soup

1 ½ cups uncooked regular long-grain white rice

3 cups water

½ cup sour cream

2 tablespoons chopped fresh chives, if desired

$**1.90** *per serving*

1 Spray 2- to 3-quart slow cooker with cooking spray. In cooker, mix beef strips and soup mix until evenly coated. Top with mushrooms and soup.

2 Cover; cook on Low heat setting 7 to 8 hours.

3 About 30 minutes before serving, cook rice in water as directed on package. Just before serving, stir sour cream into beef mixture. Sprinkle with chives. Serve over rice.

1 Serving (1 ½ cups): Calories 370; Total Fat 9g (Saturated Fat 4g; Trans Fat 0g); Cholesterol 85mg; Sodium 450mg; Total Carbohydrate 39g (Dietary Fiber 1g) **Exchanges:** 2 Starch, ½ Other Carbohydrate, 3 ½ Lean Meat **Carbohydrate Choices:** 2 ½

$mart $avings

Chives add color and flavor, but you can use some chopped green onions or green bell pepper on top instead. Fat-free mushroom soup and sour cream work well in this recipe to reduce the fat.

Pot Roast Steak and Vegetables

Pot roast has always been considered an economical meal because you start with a less tender cut of beef; just add a few vegetables, and you have a hearty one-dish meal. And it's a great way to "sneak" those veggies to the family.

Prep Time: 25 Minutes | **Start to Finish:** 8 Hours 25 Minutes | 4 servings

1 tablespoon all-purpose flour

½ teaspoon salt

⅛ teaspoon pepper

1½ lb boneless beef top round steak (½ to ¾ inch thick), trimmed of fat

4 medium potatoes, peeled, each cut into 6 pieces

4 large carrots, cut into 1-inch pieces

1 medium onion, thinly sliced

1 dried bay leaf

1 can (14 oz) beef broth (1¾ cups)

1 teaspoon Worcestershire sauce

2 tablespoons cornstarch

$3.06 *per serving*

1 In shallow bowl, mix flour, salt and pepper. Cut beef into 4 equal pieces; add to flour mixture. Turn to coat both sides. Spray 10-inch skillet with cooking spray; heat over medium-high heat. Add beef; cook 4 to 6 minutes, turning once, until browned. Remove beef from skillet; cover to keep warm.

2 Spray 3- to 4-quart slow cooker with cooking spray. In cooker, mix potatoes, carrots and onion. Add bay leaf. Place browned beef over vegetables. In small bowl, mix 1½ cups of the broth (reserve and refrigerate remaining ¼ cup broth) and the Worcestershire sauce. Pour over beef.

3 Cover; cook on Low heat setting 8 to 10 hours.

4 With slotted spoon, remove beef and vegetables from cooker; place on serving platter. Cover to keep warm.

5 Pour liquid from cooker into 2-quart saucepan; discard bay leaf. In small bowl, mix reserved ¼ cup broth and the cornstarch until smooth. Add to liquid in saucepan. Heat to boiling over medium-high heat, stirring constantly. Boil and stir 1 minute. Serve sauce over beef and vegetables.

1 Serving: Calories 420; Total Fat 6g (Saturated Fat 2g; Trans Fat 0g); Cholesterol 90mg; Sodium 790mg; Total Carbohydrate 52g (Dietary Fiber 7g) **Exchanges:** 3 Starch, 1 Vegetable, 4 Very Lean Meat, ½ Fat **Carbohydrate Choices:** 3 ½

$mart $avings

You can use 1½ pounds lean boneless beef shoulder or chuck roast for this recipe. Cut the roast into 4 equal pieces. Trim away any fat before coating the beef pieces with flour. If you have baby-cut carrots, use about 3 cups for the carrots.

Vegetable
Beef Soup

Homemade soup is comfort food that is an affordable meal when made with a less-tender cut of meat and packed with vegetables.

Prep Time: 10 Minutes | **Start to Finish:** 7 Hours 40 Minutes | 6 servings

1 lb beef stew meat, cut into bite-size pieces if necessary

1/2 lb small red potatoes, each cut into 8 pieces (about 1 1/2 cups)

1 medium onion, chopped (1/2 cup)

4 cloves garlic, finely chopped

1 teaspoon seasoned salt

1/2 teaspoon pepper

2 dried bay leaves

1 carton (32 oz) beef broth (4 cups)

1 can (14.5 oz) diced tomatoes, undrained

1 can (15 to 16 oz) great northern beans, drained, rinsed

2 cups frozen mixed vegetables, thawed

$**1.85** *per serving*

1 In 3- to 4-quart slow cooker, mix all ingredients except mixed vegetables.

2 Cover; cook on Low heat setting 7 to 8 hours.

3 Add mixed vegetables. Increase heat setting to High. Cover; cook 20 to 30 minutes longer or until vegetables are crisp-tender. Remove bay leaves before serving.

1 Serving (1 1/2 cups): Calories 330; Total Fat 10g (Saturated Fat 3.5g; Trans Fat 0g); Cholesterol 45mg; Sodium 950mg; Total Carbohydrate 35g (Dietary Fiber 8g) **Exchanges:** 1 1/2 Starch, 1/2 Other Carbohydrate, 1 Vegetable, 2 1/2 Lean Meat, 1/2 Fat **Carbohydrate Choices:** 2

$mart $avings

Watch the sales for other less tender cuts of meat, such as chuck roast or bottom round steak, that would also be great for this soup. Mixed vegetables add variety and color to the soup, but you can use other thawed, frozen veggies such as green beans or corn. Or, add a couple of sliced carrots with the potatoes.

Low   High

Off   Auto

Au Gratin Potatoes and Ham

Fresh potatoes plus some "planned over" ham make an economical family-friendly dinner. Serve with green beans, if desired.

Prep Time: 20 Minutes | **Start to Finish:** 7 Hours 20 Minutes | 7 servings

6 medium potatoes, peeled, cut into ¼-inch slices (6 cups)

1 medium onion, coarsely chopped (½ cup)

1½ cups cubed cooked ham

1 cup shredded American cheese (4 oz)

1 can (10¾ oz) condensed 98% fat-free cream of mushroom soup with 30% less sodium

½ cup milk

¼ teaspoon dried thyme leaves

$0.96 *per serving*

1 Spray 3½- to 4-quart slow cooker with cooking spray. In cooker, layer half each of the potatoes, onion, ham and cheese; repeat layers. In small bowl, mix soup, milk and thyme; pour over top.

2 Cover; cook on High heat setting 1 hour.

3 Reduce heat setting to Low. Cook 6 to 8 hours longer or until potatoes are tender.

1 Serving (1 cup): Calories 350; Total Fat 9g (Saturated Fat 4.5g; Trans Fat 0g); Cholesterol 35mg; Sodium 860mg; Total Carbohydrate 52g (Dietary Fiber 5g) **Exchanges:** 2½ Starch, 1 Other Carbohydrate, 1 High-Fat Meat **Carbohydrate Choices:** 3½

$mart $avings

Use any canned cream soup that you have on your pantry shelf, such as cream of chicken or celery. The American cheese gives a nice cheesy flavor and color, but use any cheese such as Cheddar, mozzarella or Monterey Jack cheese. Or if you have shredded Italian blend cheese in the fridge, omit the dried thyme and use it instead of the American cheese.

Easy
Barbecue
Pork
Sandwiches

Give these shredded pork sandwiches a "southern" twist by topping each serving with some of your favorite homemade creamy coleslaw or deli-purchased coleslaw.

Prep Time: 10 Minutes | **Start to Finish:** 8 Hours 10 Minutes | 6 sandwiches

½ cup barbecue sauce

½ cup sweet-and-sour sauce

1 clove garlic, finely chopped

2 lb boneless country-style pork ribs, trimmed of fat, cut into 2-inch pieces

6 kaiser rolls or burger buns, split

$**1.76** per serving

1   Spray 3 ½- to 4-quart slow cooker with cooking spray. In cooker, mix both sauces and the garlic. Stir in pork to coat.

2   Cover; cook on Low heat setting 8 to 10 hours.

3   Remove pork from slow cooker; place on plate. Shred pork by pulling apart with 2 forks. Return pork to sauce in slow cooker; mix well. If desired, to toast rolls, place cut sides up on ungreased cookie sheet; broil 4 to 6 inches from heat 1 to 2 minutes or until toasted. Spoon about ½ cup pork mixture into each roll.

1 Sandwich: Calories 490; Total Fat 20g (Saturated Fat 7g; Trans Fat 0.5g); Cholesterol 95mg; Sodium 630mg; Total Carbohydrate 41g (Dietary Fiber 1g) **Exchanges:** 1 ½ Starch, 1 Other Carbohydrate, 4 Medium-Fat Meat **Carbohydrate Choices:** 3

$mart $avings

The sweet-and-sour sauce adds a nice flavor to the pork, but if you don't have any, increase the barbecue sauce to 1 cup. For a casual get-together, stretch the number of servings by making barbecue pork sliders. Use 12 mini buns (also known as dollar buns or turkey buns), and put about ¼ cup pork on each.

Pulled Pork Sandwiches with Avocado-Onion Slaw

This isn't your ordinary pulled pork sandwich because it's topped with an avocado-onion slaw which adds creaminess as well as crunch.

Prep Time: 25 Minutes | **Start to Finish:** 7 Hours 25 Minutes | 6 servings

1 tablespoon vegetable oil

1 lb boneless pork shoulder roast, trimmed

3/4 cup chunky-style mild salsa

1 teaspoon chili powder

3/4 teaspoon ground cumin

3 tablespoons mayonnaise or salad dressing

1 tablespoon white vinegar

1/4 teaspoon salt

1 medium avocado, cubed

1/2 cup halved and thinly sliced onion

12 small flour tortillas or taco shells

1/4 cup chopped cilantro

$1.61 *per serving*

1 Spray 4-quart slow cooker with cooking spray. In 10-inch skillet, heat oil over medium heat. Cook pork in oil 6 to 8 minutes or until brown on both sides. Place pork in cooker. Cover; cook on Low heat setting 7 to 8 hours.

2 Remove pork from cooker; shred pork. Reserve 1/4 cup liquid in cooker; discard remaining liquid. Stir pork, salsa, chili powder and cumin into liquid in cooker.

3 In medium bowl, stir together mayonnaise, vinegar and salt. Gently stir in avocado and onion. To serve, place pork in tortillas; top with avocado-onion slaw and chopped cilantro.

1 Serving: Calories 430; Total Fat 25g (Saturated Fat 6g; Trans Fat 1.5g); Cholesterol 50mg; Sodium 770mg; Total Carbohydrate 31g (Dietary Fiber 3g) **Exchanges:** 2 Starch, 2 Lean Meat, 3 1/2 Fat **Carbohydrate Choices:** 2

$mart $avings

For those who are not avocado fans, try diced tomato or shredded lettuce in its place. If you have no chili powder or cumin on hand, substitute 1 3/4 teaspoons taco seasoning mix (from 1-ounce package) in their place.

Curried Lentil
Soup

Lentil soup makes a healthy lunch, so tuck a container of leftover soup in your lunch bag. Add a little water, reheat and enjoy—and enjoy saving money by not purchasing lunch.

Prep Time: 15 Minutes | **Start to Finish:** 8 Hours 15 Minutes | 8 servings

1   lb dried lentils, sorted, rinsed (2 ½ cups)

8   cups water

2   medium carrots, cut into ½-inch slices (1 cup)

2   medium stalks celery, cut into ½-inch slices (1 cup)

1   medium onion, chopped (½ cup)

2   cloves garlic, finely chopped

2   extra-large vegetarian vegetable bouillon cubes or 2 chicken bouillon cubes

3   teaspoons curry powder

1   teaspoon salt

2   bay leaves

1   can (14.5 oz) diced tomatoes, undrained

2   cups coarsely chopped fresh spinach

½   cup low-fat plain yogurt

$0.70 *per serving*

1   In 3 ½- to 4-quart slow cooker, mix all ingredients except tomatoes, spinach and yogurt.

2   Cover; cook on Low heat setting 8 to 9 hours.

3   About 5 minutes before serving, stir tomatoes into soup. Cover; cook 5 minutes longer or until thoroughly heated.

4   Just before serving, remove and discard bay leaves. Top individual servings with ¼ cup spinach and 1 tablespoon yogurt.

1 Serving (1 ½ cups): Calories 230; Total Fat 1g (Saturated Fat 0g; Trans Fat 0g); Cholesterol 0mg; Sodium 710mg; Total Carbohydrate 39g (Dietary Fiber 11g) **Exchanges:** 2 Starch, 1 Vegetable, 1 Lean Meat **Carbohydrate Choices:** 2 ½

$mart $avings

Lentils are economical and rich in protein, so they're a great main dish for dinner. Because acidic ingredients (such as tomatoes) prevent lentils from cooking until they are tender, the tomatoes are added after the lentils have cooked completely.

Barley and Sweet Potato Risotto

Add a new twist to risotto, an Italian classic rice dish, by using barley. It becomes a hearty main dish with the addition of sweet potatoes and protein-rich edamame.

Prep Time: 20 Minutes | **Start to Finish:** 4 Hours 50 Minutes | 6 servings

1   teaspoon olive or vegetable oil

3   medium sweet onions, chopped (1 1/2 cups)

3   medium cloves garlic, finely chopped

2   medium dark-orange sweet potatoes (about 12 oz), peeled, finely chopped (about 3 1/2 cups)

1 1/4 cups uncooked regular pearl barley

1   teaspoon dried thyme leaves

1/2 teaspoon salt

1   carton (32 oz) chicken broth or vegetable broth (4 cups)

1   cup frozen shelled edamame (green) soybeans (from 12-oz bag), thawed

2   tablespoons shredded Parmesan cheese

$1.17 *per serving*

1   In 10-inch nonstick skillet, heat oil over medium heat. Add onions; cook about 5 minutes, stirring occasionally, until translucent. Add garlic; cook, stirring frequently, until softened.

2   Spray 3- to 4-quart slow cooker with cooking spray. In cooker, mix sweet potatoes, barley, thyme, salt and 3 cups of the broth. Add onion-garlic mixture.

3   Cover; cook on Low heat setting 4 to 5 hours.

4   In 2-cup microwavable measuring cup, microwave remaining 1 cup broth on High 2 to 3 minutes or until boiling. Stir edamame and boiling broth into barley mixture in cooker. Increase heat setting to High. Cover; cook 25 to 30 minutes longer or until edamame are tender. Serve in large bowls; sprinkle with cheese.

1 Serving (1 1/3 cups): Calories 290; Total Fat 3.5g (Saturated Fat 1g; Trans Fat 0g); Cholesterol 0mg; Sodium 830mg; Total Carbohydrate 54g (Dietary Fiber 10g) **Exchanges:** 3 Starch, 1 Vegetable, 1/2 Fat **Carbohydrate Choices:** 3 1/2

$mart $avings

Plan to use any leftover barley risotto as a delicious side dish for beef, pork or chicken. It's easy to reheat in the microwave. Just stir in some broth or water when reheating so it becomes moist and creamy.

CHAPTER 3

Eating Out at Home

There's this great, cozy little place where the service comes with a smile, reservations aren't necessary, and there's not a bad table in the house. Your house. Best of all? The food's to-die-for and the check's always well within the budget.

Home-Cooked Special

Advantages to keeping more meals in-house start with significant cost savings and then just keep on going. There's never a wait and rarely a noisy crowd. Plus it is, by every definition, homier.

Home-Style Happy Hour Stay in for cocktails with friends. After all, the price of one or two drinks at a bar could cover a store-bought bottle of wine or six-pack of beer.

Potluck Party Rather than dining out with friends, offer up your place. Asking others to bring their specialty dishes doesn't just flatter, it cuts your cost and workload. Going appetizer-only keeps things super simple. (See Chapter 5 for ideas.)

Special Night In Instead of celebrating anniversaries, birthdays or accomplishments at pricey restaurants, eat in. Add restaurant touches to keep things special—nicely folded napkins, a well-garnished plate, a carafe of water, candlelight or your favorite background music.

Check, Please

You don't have to give up eating out completely. Instead, try these great tricks to help you get more for your money when you do.

Get Happy Restaurant happy-hours often include substantial food specials that can easily serve as your main meal. Look for midweek nightly specials, too, designed to drum up business during characteristically slow days.

Impress Yourself Order something you can't make at home. The biggest bang for your buck comes in the form of a satisfying experience you could not—or would not—re-create in your own kitchen.

Two-for-One There is no prize for cleaning your plate. Take part of your meal home and eat it as-is or re-purposed into a new meal later in the week.

Save Paper Search for restaurant coupons in your mail, in the paper, online and on the back of your grocery receipts.

Skillet Chicken Divan

Watch for chicken breasts on sale and stock up to enjoy this quick-and-easy variation of the classic Turkey Divan often.

Prep Time: 35 Minutes | **Start to Finish:** 35 Minutes | 4 servings

1 tablespoon butter or margarine

4 boneless skinless chicken breasts (about 1 1/4 lb)

1 1/4 cups water

2 tablespoons Dijon mustard

1/4 teaspoon salt

1/8 teaspoon pepper

1 cup uncooked quick-cooking brown rice

3 cups frozen broccoli florets, thawed

1/2 cup shredded Cheddar or American cheese (2 oz)

$2.35 *per serving*

1 In 10-inch nonstick skillet, melt butter over medium-high heat. Add chicken; cook 1 to 2 minutes on each side or until browned.

2 Remove chicken from skillet. Add water, mustard, salt and pepper to skillet, stirring with whisk until blended. Heat to boiling. Stir in rice; return to boiling. Place chicken pieces and broccoli over rice. Reduce heat to low; cover and simmer about 10 minutes or until most of liquid is absorbed and juice of chicken is clear when center of thickest part is cut (170°F).

3 Sprinkle with cheese; cover and let stand 5 minutes.

1 Serving: Calories 410; Total Fat 13g (Saturated Fat 6g, Trans Fat 0g); Cholesterol 95mg; Sodium 530mg; Total Carbohydrate 39g (Dietary Fiber 6g) **Exchanges:** 2 1/2 Starch, 1 Vegetable, 3 Very Lean Meat, 2 Fat **Carbohydrate Choices:** 2 1/2

$mart $avings

If you have instant white rice on hand, use it instead of the brown rice. Increase the water to 1 1/2 cups and the rice to 1 1/2 cups. Shredded Swiss cheese would also be tasty instead of the Cheddar cheese.

Grilled Fiesta Chicken Sandwiches

Grilled chicken sandwiches are a standard item on many restaurant menus, but with a little help from your grill, you can easily duplicate them at home.

Prep Time: 30 Minutes | **Start to Finish:** 30 Minutes | 4 sandwiches

- 4 **boneless skinless chicken breasts (about 1 1/4 lb)**
- 1/4 **cup grated Parmesan cheese**
- 2 **tablespoons taco seasoning mix (from 1-oz package)**
- 4 **slices (1/2 oz each) pepper Jack or Monterey Jack cheese**
- 4 **kaiser rolls or burger buns, split**
- 1/4 **cup mayonnaise or salad dressing**
- 1/4 **head iceberg lettuce, shredded (1 1/4 cups)**
- 4 **slices onion, about 1/4 inch thick**
- 1/4 **cup chunky-style salsa**

$2.03 *per serving*

1 Spray grill rack with cooking spray; place on grill. Heat gas or charcoal grill.

2 Between pieces of plastic wrap or waxed paper, place each chicken breast smooth side down; gently pound with flat side of meat mallet or rolling pin until 1/4 inch thick. In shallow bowl, mix Parmesan cheese and taco seasoning mix; coat both sides of chicken with cheese mixture.

3 Place chicken on grill over medium heat. Cover grill; cook 6 to 8 minutes, turning once, until no longer pink in center. Top each with slice of cheese; cook 1 minute longer or until cheese is melted. If desired, toast buns, cut sides down, on grill during last 1 to 2 minutes of cook time.

4 Spread mayonnaise on bottom halves of rolls. Top each with lettuce, onion, chicken and salsa; top with remaining halves of rolls.

1 Sandwich: Calories 220; Total Fat 6g (Saturated Fat 2.5g; Trans Fat 0g); Cholesterol 45mg; Sodium 610mg; Total Carbohydrate 21g (Dietary Fiber 0g) **Exchanges:** 1 1/2 Starch, 2 Very Lean Meat, 1 Fat **Carbohydrate Choices:** 1 1/2

Broiled Fiesta Chicken Sandwiches: Set oven control to broil. Spray broiler rack with cooking spray; place in broiler pan. After coating chicken with cheese mixture, place on broiler pan. Broil with tops 4 to 6 inches from heat 6 to 8 minutes or until juice of chicken is clear when center of thickest part is cut (170°F). Top each with slice of cheese; broil until cheese is melted. Continue as directed in step 4.

$mart $avings

If you prefer a plain grilled chicken sandwich, omit the Parmesan cheese and taco seasoning mix, and grill the chicken with a little salt and pepper. This sandwich is versatile, so check the fridge and pantry for what's on hand, and create your own unique sandwich. Use pesto sauce for the mayo and any leftover bruschetta mixture for the salsa. Or add some chopped chipotle chiles or green chiles to the mayo, and top each sandwich with a couple of crisp bacon strips—the options are endless.

Chicken Saltimbocca

Literally translated, *saltimbocca* means "jump in the mouth" in Italian, and this tasty chicken will do just that! Serve with string beans on the side, if desired.

Prep Time: 30 Minutes | **Start to Finish:** 30 Minutes | 4 servings

4 **boneless skinless chicken breasts (about 1 $\frac{1}{4}$ lb)**

$\frac{1}{3}$ **cup all-purpose flour**

2 **tablespoons grated Parmesan cheese**

1 **teaspoon Italian seasoning**

$\frac{1}{2}$ **teaspoon salt**

2 **tablespoons olive or vegetable oil**

4 **slices prosciutto (about 3 oz)**

4 **slices (about $\frac{3}{4}$ oz each) mozzarella cheese**

1 **teaspoon chopped fresh sage leaves**

$\frac{3}{4}$ **cup chicken broth (from 32-oz carton)**

1 **tablespoon butter or margarine**

$^\$2.52$ *per serving*

1 Between pieces of plastic wrap or waxed paper, place each chicken breast smooth side down; gently pound with flat side of meat mallet or rolling pin until $\frac{1}{4}$ inch thick. In shallow dish, mix flour, Parmesan cheese, Italian seasoning and salt. Coat chicken with flour mixture; shake off excess flour.

2 In 12-inch nonstick skillet, heat oil over medium-high heat. Add chicken; cook about 8 minutes, turning once, until browned on outside and no longer pink in center. Top each chicken breast with 1 slice prosciutto and 1 slice mozzarella cheese. Cover skillet tightly; cook 1 to 2 minutes or until cheese is melted. Sprinkle sage over chicken. Remove chicken from skillet to serving platter; cover loosely with tent of foil, being careful not to let foil touch cheese.

3 Increase heat to high. Add broth to skillet. Heat to boiling, scraping up any browned bits from bottom of skillet. Boil about 3 minutes or until broth is reduced to about $\frac{1}{4}$ cup. Remove from heat; beat in butter. Spoon over chicken.

1 Serving: Calories 460; Total Fat 24g (Saturated Fat 9g; Trans Fat 0g); Cholesterol 140mg; Sodium 1130mg; Total Carbohydrate 9g (Dietary Fiber 0g) **Exchanges:** $\frac{1}{2}$ Starch, 7 Lean Meat, $\frac{1}{2}$ Fat **Carbohydrate Choices:** $\frac{1}{2}$

$mart $avings

Prosciutto is an Italian ham that has been seasoned, salt-cured (but not smoked) and air-dried and can be relatively expensive. If you like, use less expensive thinly sliced ham for the prosciutto. Other sliced cheese, such as provolone or fontina, also goes well with the prosciutto and sage.

Stir-Fry Chicken and Asparagus

Stir-fry dishes are fun and easy when using Asian sauces and fresh ingredients, so why not enjoy stir-frying at home rather than going out?

Prep Time: 25 Minutes | **Start to Finish:** 25 Minutes | 4 servings

1 cup uncooked regular long-grain white rice

2 cups water

2 tablespoons vegetable oil

1 lb boneless skinless chicken breasts, cut into strips for stir-frying

1 lb asparagus spears, cut into 2-inch pieces

1 medium onion, cut into ½-inch wedges

8 oz fresh mushrooms, sliced (3 cups)

¼ cup water

½ cup stir-fry sauce

¼ cup oyster sauce

$3.22 *per serving*

1 In 2-quart saucepan, heat rice and water to boiling over medium-high heat. Reduce heat to low. Cover and simmer 15 minutes or until water is absorbed.

2 Meanwhile, in 12-inch skillet or wok, heat 1 tablespoon of the oil over medium-high heat until hot. Add chicken; cook and stir 5 to 6 minutes or until no longer pink in center. Remove chicken from skillet; place on plate.

3 Add remaining 1 tablespoon oil to skillet. Add asparagus and onion; cook and stir 3 minutes. Add mushrooms; cook and stir 3 minutes. Add water; cover and cook 2 to 3 minutes or until asparagus is tender.

4 Meanwhile, in small bowl, blend stir-fry sauce and oyster sauce. Return chicken to wok and add sauce mixture; cook and stir 1 minute or until hot. Serve over warm rice.

1 Serving: Calories 460; Total Fat 11g (Saturated Fat 2.5g; Trans Fat 0g); Cholesterol 70mg; Sodium 1550mg; Total Carbohydrate 56g (Dietary Fiber 3g) **Exchanges:** 3 Starch, 2 Vegetable, 3 Lean Meat **Carbohydrate Choices:** 4

$mart $avings

Oyster sauce is an Asian table condiment and stir-fry seasoning made from oysters, brine and soy sauce. If you prefer not to purchase a bottle, you can use 2 tablespoons soy sauce instead. When other mushrooms are plentiful at the market, such as shiitakes or cremini, use them in place of some or all of the regular mushrooms.

Thai Peanut Chicken and Noodles

Peanut butter and egg noodles may be staples in your pantry so with the addition of some fresh veggies and seasoning, these staples are easily turned into a flavorful Thai treat.

Prep Time: 30 Minutes | **Start to Finish:** 30 Minutes | 5 servings

- 2 ³/₄ cups uncooked fine egg noodles (6 oz)
- ¹/₄ cup creamy peanut butter
- ¹/₂ teaspoon finely chopped gingerroot
- ¹/₄ teaspoon crushed red pepper flakes
- ¹/₄ cup soy sauce
- ¹/₄ cup water
- 1 tablespoon vegetable oil
- 2 cups small fresh broccoli florets
- 1 ¹/₂ cups sliced fresh mushrooms (4 oz)
- 1 cup ready-to-eat baby-cut carrots, quartered lengthwise
- 1 medium bell pepper (any color), cut into thin bite-size strips
- 1 package (9 oz) frozen diced cooked chicken, thawed
- ¹/₄ cup coarsely chopped dry-roasted peanuts

$**1.75** *per serving*

1 Cook and drain noodles as directed on package; cover to keep warm.

2 Meanwhile, in small bowl, beat peanut butter, gingerroot, pepper flakes and 2 tablespoons of the soy sauce with whisk until blended. Gradually beat in remaining 2 tablespoons soy sauce and the water until smooth. Set aside.

3 In 12-inch nonstick skillet, heat oil over medium-high heat. Cook broccoli, mushrooms, carrots and bell pepper in oil 4 to 6 minutes, stirring occasionally, until vegetables are crisp-tender. Add chicken; cook and stir until hot.

4 Reduce heat to medium. Stir peanut butter mixture; stir into mixture in skillet. Stir in cooked noodles until coated. Cook and stir until hot. Sprinkle with peanuts.

1 Serving: Calories 380; Total Fat 17g (Saturated Fat 3g, Trans Fat 0g); Cholesterol 55mg; Sodium 900mg; Total Carbohydrate 34g (Dietary Fiber 4g) **Exchanges:** 2 Starch, 1 Vegetable, 2 Lean Meat, 2 Fat **Carbohydrate Choices:** 2

Thai Peanut Tofu and Noodles: Omit the chicken and use 1 package (12.3 oz) firm or extra-firm tofu, cut into ³/₄-inch cubes. In step 3, gently cook and stir the tofu in oil until it is lightly browned; remove from skillet. Continue as directed except gently stir in the tofu at the end of step 4. Sprinkle with peanuts and, if desired, cilantro.

$mart $avings

If you have cooked chicken on hand, there is no need to buy a package of diced chicken. Use about 1 ¹/₂ cups diced leftover chicken instead. This is a great recipe to use those few extra fresh veggies like snap peas, cauliflower florets, cut-up asparagus or sliced zucchini.

Beef with Broccoli

Beef with broccoli is a restaurant favorite that you can easily make at home—and it's easy on the budget.

Prep Time: 35 Minutes | **Start to Finish:** 35 Minutes | 4 servings

2   cups uncooked instant brown rice

1 ³/₄   cups water

1   cup beef broth

1   tablespoon cornstarch

2   tablespoons soy sauce

1   teaspoon packed brown sugar

1   tablespoon olive or vegetable oil

1   teaspoon freshly grated gingerroot

1   lb boneless beef round or tip steak, thinly sliced

1   small onion, thinly sliced (¹/₂ cup)

   Salt and pepper, if desired

¹/₂   lb fresh broccoli florets and peeled stems, cut into bite-size pieces (about 2 cups)

$2.52 *per serving*

1   Cook rice in water as directed on package. Meanwhile, in small bowl, mix broth, cornstarch, soy sauce and brown sugar. Stir until cornstarch is dissolved.

2   In 12-inch nonstick skillet, heat oil over medium-high heat. Add gingerroot, beef and onion; sprinkle with salt and pepper. Cook 2 to 4 minutes, stirring occasionally, until beef is brown. Remove beef mixture from skillet; cover to keep warm.

3   Add broth mixture and broccoli to skillet. Heat to boiling; reduce heat. Cook 5 to 10 minutes or until sauce thickens and broccoli is tender. Return beef mixture to skillet; cook until hot, stirring occasionally. Serve over warm rice.

1 Serving: Calories 590; Total Fat 11g (Saturated Fat 2.5g, Trans Fat 0g); Cholesterol 85mg; Sodium 1030mg; Total Carbohydrate 80g (Dietary Fiber 12g) **Exchanges:** 5 Starch, 1 Vegetable, 3 Lean Meat **Carbohydrate Choices:** 5

Pork with Broccoli: Substitute 1 lb pork tenderloin, thinly sliced, for the beef round steak and 1 cup chicken broth for the beef broth.

$mart $avings

Round steak is a less expensive cut of beef but is less tender than some more expensive steaks. Because the steak is cut into thin slices for this stir-fry dish, it doesn't require the usual long cook time and is tender within minutes.

Grilled Flank Steak Salad with Parmesan Crisps

Slices of tender steak on a bed of crisp salad greens is a great way to stretch a pound of steak without stretching the budget. The Parmesan Crisps add that special restaurant touch.

Prep Time: 45 Minutes | **Start to Finish:** 2 Hours 45 Minutes | 4 servings

1 lb beef flank steak

½ cup balsamic vinaigrette dressing or Italian dressing

6 tablespoons finely shredded Parmesan cheese

¼ teaspoon cracked black pepper

1 lb fresh asparagus spears, trimmed

¼ teaspoon salt

⅛ teaspoon pepper

6 cups bite-size pieces romaine lettuce (1 lb)

12 medium radishes, thinly sliced (½ cup)

Additional ¼ cup dressing

$4.41 *per serving*

1 In large nonmetal dish, place steak and ½ cup dressing; turn to coat. Cover dish; refrigerate at least 2 hours but no longer than 24 hours to marinate.

2 Heat oven to 350°F. Spray large cookie sheet with cooking spray. To make Parmesan Crisps, spoon heaping teaspoonfuls cheese in 12 mounds on cookie sheet. Spread each into 2-inch circle. Bake 6 to 8 minutes or until light brown. Carefully remove from pan to cooling rack. (Crisps may be made up to 2 days ahead and kept between layers of waxed paper in airtight container at room temperature.)

3 Heat gas or charcoal grill. Remove steak from marinade; reserve marinade. Sprinkle steak with pepper. Place steak on grill over medium heat. Cover grill; cook 15 to 18 minutes or until desired doneness, turning halfway through grilling. Let stand 5 minutes.

4 Meanwhile, toss asparagus with reserved marinade. Place asparagus in grill basket (grill "wok"); discard any remaining marinade. Place asparagus on grill. Cover grill; cook 6 to 8 minutes, turning occasionally, until tender. Sprinkle asparagus with salt and pepper.

5 In large bowl, toss lettuce, radishes and the additional ¼ cup dressing. Divide lettuce mixture among 4 dinner plates. Cut steak across grain into thin slices. Divide steak slices and asparagus evenly among plates. Serve with crisps.

1 Serving: Calories 440; Total Fat 29g (Saturated Fat 6g; Trans Fat 0g); Cholesterol 90mg; Sodium 700mg; Total Carbohydrate 6g (Dietary Fiber 3g) **Exchanges:** 1 Vegetable, 5 Lean Meat, 3 Fat **Carbohydrate Choices:** ½

Broiled Flank Steak with Parmesan Crisps: Follow steps 1 and 2 as directed. Set oven control to broil. Remove steak from marinade; sprinkle with pepper. Place on broiler pan. Broil with top 2 to 3 inches from heat 12 to 14 minutes or until desired doneness, turning halfway through broiling. Let stand 5 minutes. Cook asparagus under broiler just until tender; sprinkle with salt and pepper. Continue as directed in step 5.

Making the Parmesan **Crisps**

Shanghai Sliders

Sliders are appearing on menus everywhere, from fine-dining restaurants to fast-food chains. Enjoy these Asian-style sliders as a meal or serve as an appetizer at your next party.

Prep Time: 35 Minutes | **Start to Finish:** 35 Minutes | 8 servings

Topping

- 4 small yellow onions, thinly sliced (about 2 cups)
- 1 cup reduced-sodium chicken broth (from 32-oz carton)
- ¼ cup dry sherry or apple juice
- ¼ cup soy sauce
- 1 tablespoon sugar
- 2 (¼-inch) slices fresh gingerroot

Patties

- 1 cup ketchup
- 2 teaspoons roasted red chili paste, if desired
- 1½ lb lean (at least 80%) ground beef
- 4 medium green onions, finely chopped (¼ cup)
- 1 tablespoon finely chopped gingerroot
- 1 teaspoon garlic salt
- 16 mini burger buns (2½ inches in diameter), split

$1.25 per serving

1 In 10-inch skillet, mix topping ingredients. Heat to boiling over high heat, stirring occasionally. Reduce heat to medium-low; simmer about 15 minutes or until onions are softened and liquid is reduced by half. Remove gingerroot slices.

2 Meanwhile, in small bowl, mix ketchup and chili paste; set aside. In large bowl, mix beef, green onions, 1 tablespoon gingerroot and the garlic salt with hands just until blended. Divide mixture into 16 equal portions. Using wet hands, shape each portion into patty, about ¼ inch thick.

3 Heat 12-inch nonstick skillet over medium-high heat. Add patties; cook 3 to 4 minutes on each side, pressing patties down lightly with spatula to flatten before turning over, until meat thermometer inserted in center of patties reads 160°F.

4 Place patties on bottoms of buns. Top patties with ketchup mixture. Using slotted spoon or fork, remove onion slices from skillet; place on top of ketchup mixture. Top with tops of buns.

1 Serving (2 sandwiches): Calories 350; Total Fat 12g (Saturated Fat 4g; Trans Fat 1g); Cholesterol 55mg; Sodium 1250mg; Total Carbohydrate 38g (Dietary Fiber 2g) **Exchanges:** 1½ Starch, ½ Other Carbohydrate, 1 Vegetable, 2 Medium-Fat Meat, ½ Fat **Carbohydrate Choices:** 2½

Shanghai Burgers: Prepare as directed in steps 1 and 2—except shape the beef mixture into 6 patties, about ¾ inch thick. Cook 12 to 15 minutes or until meat thermometer inserted in center of patties reads 160°F. Place patties on bottoms of 6 burger buns. Continue as directed in step 4.

$mart $avings

Mini buns are sometimes labeled as turkey or dollar buns. If they're not available, use split dinner rolls. If you don't have sherry or apple juice, increase the broth to 1½ cups.

Grilled Blue Cheese Burgers

Be a "home chef." Fire up the grill, and serve a platter of burgers to friends. Burgers? Yes. Mom's everyday burgers? Definitely not. Blue cheese lovers will devour these burgers because there's a dose of blue cheese in every bite.

Prep Time: 25 Minutes | **Start to Finish:** 25 Minutes | 4 sandwiches

- 1 lb lean (at least 80%) ground beef
- 1/2 cup crumbled blue cheese (2 oz)
- 1/2 teaspoon garlic powder
- 1/2 teaspoon salt
- 1/4 teaspoon pepper
- 4 onion or burger buns, split
- 4 slices tomato
- Additional crumbled blue cheese, if desired

$1.67 *per serving*

1 Heat gas or charcoal grill. In medium bowl, mix beef, 1/2 cup cheese, the garlic powder, salt and pepper. Shape mixture into 4 (4-inch) patties, about 1/2 inch thick.

2 Place patties on grill over medium heat. Cover grill; cook 11 to 13 minutes, turning once, until meat thermometer inserted in center of patties reads 160°F. If desired, toast buns, cut sides down, on grill during last 1 to 2 minutes of cook time.

3 Place patties on bottoms of buns. Top with tomato slices and additional blue cheese. Top with tops of buns.

1 Sandwich: Calories 350; Total Fat 18g (Saturated Fat 8g; Trans Fat 1g); Cholesterol 80mg; Sodium 720mg; Total Carbohydrate 19g (Dietary Fiber 1g) **Exchanges:** 1 Starch, 1/2 Other Carbohydrate, 3 Medium-Fat Meat, 1/2 Fat **Carbohydrate Choices:** 1

Broiled Blue Cheese Burgers: Set oven control to broil. Prepare patties as directed in step 1. Place patties on rack in broiler pan. Broil with tops 2 to 3 inches from heat 10 to 12 minutes, turning once, until meat thermometer inserted in center of patties reads 160°F. Continue as directed in step 3.

$mart $avings

One or two onions in the bottom of the bag? Slice and sauté them in butter or olive oil to top the burgers. Crumble those couple slices of leftover cooked bacon and add to the meat mixture before cooking, or sprinkle on top of each burger. If you're not a fan of blue cheese, substitute crumbled feta. No buns or tomatoes? These burgers will be just as delicious served alongside your favorite potatoes and veggie.

Beef and Green Chile Enchiladas

Enchiladas, a favorite Mexican dish, are easy to make—enjoy them anytime at home.

Prep Time: 25 Minutes | **Start to Finish:** 1 Hour 15 Minutes | 6 servings

1 lb lean (at least 80%) ground beef

1 medium onion, chopped (½ cup)

1 cup frozen whole kernel corn

½ cup sour cream

1 can (4.5 oz) chopped green chiles

1½ cups shredded Colby–Monterey Jack cheese blend (6 oz)

1 can (10 oz) enchilada sauce

6 flour tortillas (8 inch)

Shredded lettuce, if desired

Chopped tomatoes, if desired

Additional sour cream, if desired

$1.69 *per serving*

1 Heat oven to 350°F. In 10-inch nonstick skillet, cook beef and onion over medium-high heat 5 to 7 minutes, stirring occasionally, until beef is thoroughly cooked; drain. Add corn; cook and stir about 3 minutes or until corn is thawed. Stir in sour cream, chiles and ½ cup of the cheese.

2 In 13×9-inch (3-quart) glass baking dish, spread about ¼ cup of the enchilada sauce. Spread about 2 teaspoons enchilada sauce on each tortilla. Top each with ⅔ cup beef mixture. Roll up tortillas; place seam side down over enchilada sauce in baking dish.

3 Drizzle remaining enchilada sauce evenly over filled tortillas. Sprinkle with remaining 1 cup cheese. Spray sheet of foil with cooking spray; place sprayed side down on baking dish and seal tightly.

4 Bake 45 to 50 minutes or until hot. Serve with lettuce, tomatoes and additional sour cream.

1 Serving: Calories 510; Total Fat 29g (Saturated Fat 14g; Trans Fat 1.5g); Cholesterol 95mg; Sodium 1080mg; Total Carbohydrate 34g (Dietary Fiber 2g) **Exchanges:** 1 ½ Starch, ½ Other Carbohydrate, 3 ½ High-Fat Meat **Carbohydrate Choices:** 2

$mart $avings

If you have ground turkey in the freezer or it's on sale, use it for the ground beef. The corn adds a bit of color and nice texture to the filling, but if you don't have any on hand you can omit it and still have tasty enchiladas. You can top enchiladas with other toppings that you may have, such as sliced radishes, sliced olives, chopped avocado or chopped cilantro.

Four-Cheese Pasta

Four delicate-flavored cheeses, melted and bubbly, surround tender pieces of pasta topped off with crisp golden bread crumbs, creating a dish that will turn any meal into a special occasion—and it fits within the budget, too!

Prep Time: 25 Minutes | **Start to Finish:** 50 Minutes | 6 servings

16 oz uncooked penne pasta (5 cups)

½ cup butter or margarine

2 cloves garlic, finely chopped

½ cup all-purpose flour

1 teaspoon salt

4½ cups milk

1 cup shredded provolone cheese (4 oz)

1 cup shredded mozzarella cheese (4 oz)

½ cup shredded Parmesan cheese (2 oz)

½ cup shredded fontina cheese (2 oz)

⅓ cup chopped fresh parsley, if desired

1 tablespoon butter or margarine

1 cup panko bread crumbs

$**1.62** *per serving*

1 Heat oven to 350°F. Spray 13×9-inch (3-quart) glass baking dish with cooking spray. Cook and drain pasta as directed on package.

2 Meanwhile, in 4-quart saucepan or Dutch oven, melt ½ cup butter over low heat. Add garlic; cook 30 seconds, stirring frequently. With whisk, stir in flour and salt until smooth. Increase heat to medium; cook, stirring constantly, until mixture is smooth and bubbly. Gradually stir in milk. Heat to boiling, stirring constantly. Boil and stir 1 minute. Stir in cheeses. Cook until melted, stirring occasionally. Stir pasta and parsley into cheese sauce. Pour mixture into baking dish.

3 In 6-inch skillet, melt 1 tablespoon butter over medium-high heat; stir in bread crumbs. Cook and stir until crumbs are golden brown. Sprinkle over pasta mixture.

4 Bake uncovered 20 to 25 minutes or until bubbly.

1 Serving: Calories 850; Total Fat 39g (Saturated Fat 23g; Trans Fat 1g); Cholesterol 100mg; Sodium 1390mg; Total Carbohydrate 91g (Dietary Fiber 4g) **Exchanges:** 5 Starch, 1 Other Carbohydrate, 3 High-Fat Meat, 2 Fat **Carbohydrate Choices:** 6

$mart $avings

Panko bread crumbs are Japanese-style bread crumbs that have a coarser texture and make for a much lighter and crunchier casserole topping. Regular dry bread crumbs will also work, but you may want to use half the amount. The four cheeses in this recipe complement each other, but you can easily use any combination of shredded cheese that you prefer. And check the pantry for other tubular pastas that can be used for the penne.

Mostaccioli with Italian Sausage

Create a family-style Italian restaurant at home by spooning this pasta dish onto a platter. Gather the family around the table, and pass the pasta.

Prep Time: 10 Minutes | **Start to Finish:** 35 Minutes | 4 servings

- 1 tablespoon olive oil
- 2 slices uncooked bacon, cut into ½-inch pieces
- 1 medium onion, chopped (½ cup)
- ½ lb bulk Italian pork sausage
- 1 can (28 oz) diced tomatoes, undrained
- 1 jar (4.5 oz) sliced mushrooms, undrained
- ¾ cup chicken broth (from 32-oz carton)
- 1 teaspoon dried basil leaves
- ¼ teaspoon salt
- ¼ teaspoon pepper
- 4 oz uncooked mostaccioli pasta (2 cups)
- ¼ cup shredded Parmesan cheese (1 oz), if desired

$1.87 *per serving*

1 In 12-inch skillet, heat oil over medium-high heat. Add bacon, onion and sausage. Cook 4 to 7 minutes, stirring occasionally, until sausage is no longer pink; drain if necessary.

2 Stir in tomatoes, mushrooms, broth, basil, salt, pepper and pasta. Reduce heat to medium-low. Cover; cook 20 to 25 minutes, stirring occasionally, until pasta is tender. Sprinkle with cheese.

1 Serving: Calories 400; Total Fat 20g (Saturated Fat 6g; Trans Fat 0g); Cholesterol 30mg; Sodium 1330mg; Total Carbohydrate 38g (Dietary Fiber 4g) **Exchanges:** 2 Starch, 1½ Vegetable, 1 High-Fat Meat, 2 Fat **Carbohydrate Choices:** 2½

$mart $avings

You can vary the type of meat by using ½ pound ground beef or 2 uncooked chicken breasts, cut into 1-inch pieces, for the sausage. Add ¼ to ½ teaspoon Italian seasoning with the basil. A 28-ounce can of whole tomatoes can be used for the diced, and use kitchen scissors to break up the tomatoes.

Chicago Deep-Dish Sausage Pizza

Chicago-style "deep-dish" pizza is reported to have been created in a Chicago restaurant in 1943. Years later, you can still make this fabulous pizza in your own kitchen.

Prep Time: 25 Minutes | **Start to Finish:** 50 Minutes | 6 servings

1	lb bulk Italian pork sausage
1	small bell pepper (any color), chopped (½ cup)
1	cup sliced fresh mushrooms
1	can (8 oz) pizza sauce
1	can (13.8 oz) refrigerated classic pizza crust
1½	cups shredded mozzarella cheese (6 oz)
2	medium plum (Roma) tomatoes, chopped
¼	cup sliced ripe olives, if desired
2	medium green onions, chopped (2 tablespoons)

$1.86 *per serving*

1 Heat oven to 400°F. Spray 9-inch square pan with cooking spray. In 10-inch nonstick skillet, cook sausage and bell pepper over medium-high heat 7 to 9 minutes, stirring frequently, until sausage is no longer pink. Stir in mushrooms and pizza sauce. Keep warm over low heat.

2 Unroll dough; place in pan. Starting at center, press out dough to edges of pan, pressing at least 1 inch up sides, folding edge under to form crust. Sprinkle ½ cup of the cheese evenly over crust. Spoon hot sausage mixture over cheese. Top with remaining 1 cup cheese, the tomatoes and olives.

3 Bake 15 to 20 minutes or until crust is golden brown. Sprinkle with onions. Let stand 5 minutes before cutting.

1 Serving: Calories 390; Total Fat 18g (Saturated Fat 7g; Trans Fat 0g); Cholesterol 45mg; Sodium 1050mg; Total Carbohydrate 37g (Dietary Fiber 1g) **Exchanges:** 2 Starch, ½ Other Carbohydrate, 2 High-Fat Meat **Carbohydrate Choices:** 2 ½

$mart $avings

Watch for pizza crust coupons or sales so you can stock your freezer. Plum (Roma) tomatoes can be slightly more expensive but work best on pizza because they don't release as much moisture during baking.

Pepperoni Cheese-Stuffed Pizza

You can never have too much cheese when it comes to eating pizza. Not only is there melted cheese on top, but there's a hidden surprise in the edge of the crust—more cheese!

Prep Time: 15 Minutes | **Start to Finish:** 45 Minutes | 8 servings

1 can (13.8 oz) refrigerated classic pizza crust

7 sticks (1 oz each) string cheese

24 slices pepperoni (from 3.5-oz package)

½ cup pizza sauce

2 cups shredded Italian cheese blend (8 oz)

$\$1.02$ *per serving*

1 Heat oven to 425°F. Spray 12-inch pizza pan with cooking spray. Unroll dough; place in pan. Starting at center, press out dough to edge of pan, pressing up and extending over edge by at least 1 inch. Place string cheese around inside edge of crust. Fold extended edge of dough over cheese; pinch firmly to seal.

2 Bake 8 to 10 minutes or until crust is set and edges are light golden brown.

3 Remove partially baked crust from oven. Spoon sauce evenly over crust. Top with pepperoni and Italian cheese blend.

4 Bake 12 to 16 minutes longer or until crust is deep golden brown and cheese in center is melted. Cut into wedges.

1 Serving: Calories 300; Total Fat 14g (Saturated Fat 8g, Trans Fat 0g); Cholesterol 35mg; Sodium 760mg; Total Carbohydrate 26g (Dietary Fiber 1g) **Exchanges:** 1 Starch, ½ Other Carbohydrate, 2 Medium-Fat Meat, 1 Fat **Carbohydrate Choices:** 2

Stuffing the Crust Edge

$mart $avings

Any extra sticks of string cheese make a great snack or nice addition to a lunch bag. The Italian cheese blend is good on this pizza, but you can use shredded mozzarella or Monterey Jack cheese instead.

Shrimp
Scampi

Scampi is the Italian word for the tail portion of a variety of lobsterettes or prawns. On restaurant menus, scampi often refers to a dish prepared with shrimp, butter and garlic.

Prep Time: 10 Minutes | **Start to Finish:** 25 Minutes | 4 servings

- 2 **cups uncooked white or brown rice or 8 oz uncooked fettuccine**
- 2 **tablespoons butter or margarine**
- 1 **tablespoon olive oil**
- 4 **cloves garlic, finely chopped**
- 1 **lb uncooked peeled deveined medium shrimp**
- ¼ **cup chopped fresh parsley**
- 2 **teaspoons finely shredded lemon peel**
- ¼ **teaspoon salt**
- ¼ **teaspoon pepper**
- ⅓ **cup dry white wine or chicken broth**

$3.08 *per serving*

1 Cook rice or fettuccine as directed on package to desired doneness. Drain; cover and keep warm.

2 Meanwhile, in 10-inch skillet, heat butter and oil over medium heat until butter is melted. Add garlic; cook and stir 1 minute. Add shrimp; cook and stir 1 minute. Add remaining ingredients except rice or fettuccine; cook and stir 1 to 2 minutes or until shrimp are pink.

3 Serve over rice or fettuccine.

1 Serving: Calories 370; Total Fat 13g (Saturated Fat 5g, Trans Fat 0g); Cholesterol 220mg; Sodium 620mg; Total Carbohydrate 39g (Dietary Fiber 2g) **Exchanges:** 2 ½ Starch, 2 ½ Lean Meat, 1 Fat **Carbohydrate Choices:** 2 ½

$mart $avings

Serving the shrimp on a bed of rice or fettuccine helps to stretch a pound of shrimp. Sometimes bags of frozen shrimp are less expensive or on sale, which would make this dish even more affordable.

Asian
Salmon

Salmon is expensive, but treat yourself for a special occasion, and serve this Asian-flavored version at home. Serve with string beans and colorful bell peppers, if desired.

Prep Time: 45 Minutes | **Start to Finish:** 55 Minutes | 8 servings

$\frac{2}{3}$ cup teriyaki marinade and sauce

$\frac{1}{4}$ cup apricot preserves

$\frac{1}{4}$ cup water

2 tablespoons vegetable oil

4 teaspoons grated gingerroot

2 teaspoons Dijon mustard

4 medium cloves garlic, finely chopped

3 lb salmon fillets

2 medium green onions, thinly sliced (2 tablespoons)

1 tablespoon sesame seed, toasted*

$2.48 *per serving*

1 Heat oven to 425°F. Line 15×10×1-inch pan with foil; spray foil with cooking spray.

2 In 2-quart saucepan, stir together teriyaki sauce, preserves, water, oil, gingerroot, mustard and garlic. Heat to boiling over medium-high heat, stirring occasionally. Reduce heat to low; simmer uncovered about 5 minutes, stirring occasionally, until slightly thickened.

3 Cut salmon into 8 serving pieces if necessary. Place salmon, skin sides down, in pan. Spoon $\frac{1}{2}$ cup sauce mixture over salmon.

4 Bake uncovered 20 to 25 minutes, rotating pan after 10 minutes, until salmon flakes easily with fork.

5 Meanwhile, heat remaining sauce mixture to boiling. Reduce heat to low; simmer uncovered about 5 minutes, stirring occasionally, until thickened and reduced to about $\frac{1}{2}$ cup. Carefully transfer salmon to serving platter. Drizzle with thickened sauce mixture. Sprinkle with onions and sesame seed.

*To toast sesame seed, sprinkle in ungreased heavy skillet. Cook over medium-low heat 5 to 7 minutes, stirring frequently until browning begins, then stirring constantly until golden brown.

1 Serving: Calories 280; Total Fat 12g (Saturated Fat 3g; Trans Fat 0g); Cholesterol 95mg; Sodium 940mg; Total Carbohydrate 11g (Dietary Fiber 0g) **Exchanges:** 1 Other Carbohydrate, 4 Lean Meat **Carbohydrate Choices:** 1

$mart $avings

Watch for sales, and if salmon steak is less expensive per pound than fillets, use 8 (6 ounces each) steaks. This recipe is easy to cut in half if you need only 4 servings. Use a 13×9-inch pan lined with foil and sprayed with cooking spray. Lining the pan with foil makes cleanup easier; because the marinade is high in sugar and probably would bake onto the pan, you'd need a little elbow grease to get it clean!

Grilled Halibut with Chipotle Butter

Halibut, a mild-flavored fish, is popular in restaurants and can be more expensive than other fish on the menu. However, you can easily prepare it at home and enjoy a less costly meal than eating out. Add veggies on the side for a delicious addition to the meal.

Prep Time: 30 Minutes | **Start to Finish:** 30 Minutes | 4 servings

- ¼ cup butter, softened
- 1 chipotle chile in adobo sauce (from 7- or 11-oz can), chopped
- 1 teaspoon adobo sauce (from can of chipotle chiles)
- 1 teaspoon lime juice
- 2 tablespoons chopped fresh cilantro
- 1 tablespoon olive oil
- 1 teaspoon chili powder
- ½ teaspoon garlic salt
- ½ teaspoon ground cumin
- 4 halibut steaks (6 oz each)

$4.42 *per serving*

1 Heat gas or charcoal grill. In small bowl, mix butter, chile, adobo sauce, lime juice and cilantro. Refrigerate until serving time.

2 In small bowl, mix oil, chili powder, garlic salt and cumin. Brush both sides of each halibut steak with oil mixture.

3 Place halibut on grill over medium heat. Cook 10 to 15 minutes or until fish flakes easily with fork, turning once or twice. Serve halibut topped with chipotle butter.

1 Serving: Calories 260; Total Fat 17g (Saturated Fat 8g; Trans Fat 0g); Cholesterol 105mg; Sodium 380mg; Total Carbohydrate 1g (Dietary Fiber 0g) **Exchanges:** 3 ½ Lean Meat, 1 ½ Fat **Carbohydrate Choices:** 0

Broiled Halibut with Chipotle Butter: Set oven control to broil. Spray broiler rack with cooking spray. Place halibut steaks on broiler pan; broil 4 to 6 inches from heat 10 to 15 minutes or until fish flakes easily with fork, turning once or twice.

$mart $avings

If halibut isn't available or is out of your price range, check if salmon or swordfish steak is available or costs less. Chipotle chile adds a spiciness to the fish, but other flavored butters are good, too. You may want to try one of the following added to ¼ cup softened butter:

- 1 finely chopped clove garlic or ¼ teaspoon garlic powder for garlic butter

- 1 to 2 tablespoons chopped fresh herbs or 1 teaspoon dried herbs for herbed butter

- 1 tablespoon finely shredded lemon peel, ½ teaspoon lemon juice and ⅛ teaspoon pepper for lemon-pepper butter

Grilled Lemon-Thyme Tuna Steaks

Fresh tuna has become very popular on restaurant menus the last few years as an entrée or appetizer. With the help of the grill, you can make restaurant-quality tuna steaks at home.

Prep Time: 20 Minutes | **Start to Finish:** 50 Minutes | 4 servings

4   yellow fin tuna steaks, ¹/₂ inch thick (6 oz each)

¹/₄   cup olive oil

2   teaspoons finely chopped fresh thyme

1   teaspoon salt

1   teaspoon grated lemon peel

¹/₄   cup fresh lemon juice

¹/₂   teaspoon pepper

$5.08 *per serving*

1   Place tuna in nonmetal pan or shallow bowl. In small bowl, mix remaining ingredients; pour over tuna. Turn tuna over to coat both sides with marinade. Cover and refrigerate at least 30 minutes but no longer than 2 hours.

2   Spray grill rack with cooking spray. Heat gas or charcoal grill.

3   Remove tuna from marinade; discard marinade. Place tuna on grill over medium heat; cover and cook 6 to 7 minutes, turning once, until tuna flakes easily with fork and is slightly pink in center.

1 Serving: Calories 170; Total Fat 5g (Saturated Fat 1g; Trans Fat 0g); Cholesterol 80mg; Sodium 280mg; Total Carbohydrate 0g (Dietary Fiber 0g) **Exchanges:** 4 Very Lean Meat, ¹/₂ Fat **Carbohydrate Choices:** 0

Broiled Lemon-Thyme Tuna Steaks: Set oven control to broil. Spray broiler rack with cooking spray. Remove tuna steaks from marinade; discard marinade. Place tuna steaks on broiler pan; broil with tops 4 to 6 inches from heat 6 to 7 minutes or until fish flakes easily with fork and is slightly pink in center, turning once.

$mart $avings

Tuna is a firm fish, and the lemon juice helps tenderize it. However, don't marinate for more than 2 hours, or the tuna will become mushy. If you don't have fresh thyme, use ¹/₂ teaspoon dried thyme. Other fresh herbs—dill, basil, oregano, sage—also go nicely with lemon and tuna.

Fish Tacos

Fish tacos are popular on restaurant menus, and they are easy to make so you can enjoy them at home.

Prep Time: 25 Minutes | **Start to Finish:** 25 Minutes | 5 servings

2 tablespoons butter or margarine, melted

2 tablespoons 40% less-sodium taco seasoning mix (from 1-oz package)

1 lb white fish fillets, such as tilapia or catfish, about ¾ inch thick

3 tablespoons reduced-fat ranch dressing

4 cups coleslaw mix (shredded cabbage and carrots)

1 small jalapeño chile, seeded, finely chopped

10 corn tortillas (6 inch)

10 radishes, sliced (1 ¼ cups)

Red pepper sauce to taste, if desired

Tomatillo salsa, if desired

$3.15 per serving

1 Heat oven to 375°F. Spray 13×9-inch pan with cooking spray. In small bowl, mix butter with 2 teaspoons of the taco seasoning mix; brush on both sides of fish fillets. Place fish in pan (if fish has skin, place skin side down); tuck under any thin ends for more even cooking.

2 Bake uncovered 15 to 20 minutes or until fish flakes easily with fork. Let cool slightly (remove skin from fish); cut into bite-size chunks.

3 Meanwhile, in large bowl, mix dressing and remaining 4 teaspoons taco seasoning mix. Add coleslaw mix and chile; toss to coat. Let stand 10 minutes. Place tortillas between slightly dampened microwavable paper towels; microwave on High about 45 seconds or until warm.

4 To serve, spoon about ¼ cup fish chunks and ¼ cup coleslaw mixture onto each tortilla; top with 2 tablespoons radishes. Fold tortillas around filling. Serve with pepper sauce and tomatillo salsa.

1 Serving (2 tacos): Calories 240; Total Fat 4g (Saturated Fat 0.5g; Trans Fat 0g); Cholesterol 50mg; Sodium 410mg; Total Carbohydrate 30g (Dietary Fiber 4g) **Exchanges:** 1 ½ Starch, 1 Vegetable, 2 Very Lean Meat, ½ Fat **Carbohydrate Choices:** 2

Grilled Fish Tacos: Heat gas or charcoal grill. Spray 18×12-inch sheet of heavy-duty foil with cooking spray. Place sprinkled fish fillets on center of foil. Bring up 2 sides of foil so edges meet. Seal edges, making tight ½-inch fold; fold again, allowing space for heat circulation and expansion. Fold other sides to seal. Place packet on grill over high heat. Cover grill; cook about 10 minutes, rotating packet ½ turn after 5 minutes, until fish flakes easily with fork. Cool slightly; cut into bite-size pieces. Continue as directed in step 3.

$mart $avings

If you have a head of cabbage, you can use 4 cups of finely shredded cabbage for the coleslaw mix. And if you want, shred a carrot or two to mix with the cabbage (but no one will miss them if you don't). The green tomatillo salsa is a nice color change, but any red salsa will taste good, too.

CHAPTER 4

No One Will Miss the Meat

Sure, choosing meatless meals here and there saves you money. That certainly doesn't mean it's a sacrifice. Select the right recipe, and this is one of those win-win situations: Delicious, filling meal. Fantastically low cost. What's to miss when hearty comfort foods, classic ethnic dishes and other tasty favorites wait on the dinner table?

Explore the Possibilities

Meat-free tends to cost less. Zero in on the right recipes to ensure the post-dinner plates end up empty and your pocketbook stays full. Start here:

Make Breakfast for Supper Change things up. Eat your morning meal at night. Eggs, especially, make inexpensive and wonderfully protein-packed options. Consider hearty omelets, savory stratas and classic egg bakes.

Globe Trot Lots of cultures have flavorful dishes that focus on beans, grains or pastas. Think of familiars such as Italian pastas with tomato sauces and spicy Asian rice and noodle dishes.

Veg Out Simply add vegetables, fresh, frozen or canned, where you normally would have meat—think veggie lasagna or chili, for example.

Be Cheesy Cheese makes for a delicious and filling meat stand-in. Stretch more expensive favorites by combining them with rice, pasta or less-expensive processed cheeses, which also melt beautifully.

Rely on Staples Experiment with diverse rice, grains and beans, canned or dried. Not only are they inexpensive, they're also healthy and quite satisfying.

Edible Arrangement

Prolong the shelf life of fresh herbs, from store or garden, by storing them in a glass of water. Immerse just the stems, and set your herb bouquet in a sunny spot on your counter, just as you would a vase of flowers. Bonus: If you see them often, you're more likely to use them. If you prefer refrigeration, set them in an out-of-the-way spot covered with a plastic bag.

Spice It Up

It's neither meat nor money spent that makes a meal—it's flavor. Know the basics of dried herbs and spices to pinpoint your preferences, maximize freshness and find quality, low-cost combinations to make any dish sing.

In the Dark Herbs and spices keep best far away from oxygen, light and heat—time to reconsider that spice rack next to the stovetop. Tightly twist on covers.

Sub Smart Dry herbs substitute for fresh ones at a 1-to-3 ratio. On a smaller scale, remember that one tablespoon fresh equals one teaspoon dried.

Daily Grind Whole dried herbs and spices keep about twice as long as pre-ground. Consider buying whole and crushing for use with a coffee or spice grinder or mortar and pestle.

Mix Master No need to shell out more for someone else's rub or similar mix of spices. Experiment with your own flavor combinations.

Say When Sometimes, the simple duo of freshly ground pepper and salt is perfect.

Make-Ahead Vegetable-Egg Bake

Eggs are a good base for many one-dish main dishes because they're inexpensive and taste great—not only for breakfast, but dinner, too. Top servings with roasted bell pepper pieces, if desired.

Prep Time: 25 Minutes | **Start to Finish:** 9 Hours 45 Minutes | 12 servings

2   **tablespoons butter or margarine**

2   **medium leeks, quartered, sliced, using bulb and light green portions (about 2 cups)**

8   **to 10 spears fresh asparagus, trimmed, broken into 1-inch pieces (8 oz)**

5   **cups frozen southern-style hash-brown potatoes (from 32-oz package)**

$\frac{1}{2}$ **cup roasted red bell pepper strips (from 7.25-oz jar)**

1   **teaspoon salt**

1   **teaspoon dried dill weed**

8   **eggs**

1   **pint (2 cups) half-and-half or milk**

1   **cup finely shredded fresh Parmesan cheese (4 oz)**

$^{\$}$**1.04** *per serving*

1   Spray 13×9-inch (3-quart) glass baking dish with cooking spray. In 12-inch skillet, melt butter over medium-high heat. Add leeks and asparagus; cook and stir 5 to 6 minutes or until crisp-tender.

2   Add potatoes, roasted pepper strips, salt and dill; mix lightly. Spoon evenly into baking dish.

3   In medium bowl, beat eggs with whisk. Add half-and-half; beat well. Add $\frac{1}{2}$ cup of the cheese; mix well. Pour over vegetable mixture in baking dish. Sprinkle with remaining $\frac{1}{2}$ cup cheese. Cover with foil; refrigerate at least 8 hours but no longer than 24 hours.

4   Heat oven to 350°F. Bake, covered, 45 minutes. Uncover; bake 20 to 25 minutes longer or until center is set. Let stand 10 minutes. Cut into squares.

1 Serving: Calories 250; Total Fat 13g (Saturated Fat 6g; Trans Fat 1g); Cholesterol 165mg; Sodium 450mg; Total Carbohydrate 22g (Dietary Fiber 2g) **Exchanges:** 1 $\frac{1}{2}$ Starch, 1 Medium-Fat Meat, 1 $\frac{1}{2}$ Fat **Carbohydrate Choices:** 1 $\frac{1}{2}$

$mart $avings

This do-ahead dish is perfect for dinner because you can prepare it the night before or the morning of the day you want to serve it. While it bakes, you can do other chores and have a relaxing evening. Leeks have a milder flavor than onions, but it takes time to remove all the dirt. To save time, use 1 chopped large onion (1 cup) for the leeks.

Cheesy Baked Supper Omelet

Omelets aren't just for breakfast—and they're a great way to use leftovers. Add a little chopped ham or a few pieces of crumbled cooked bacon, chopped fresh dill or basil, some shredded carrot or crumbled blue cheese—it all adds flavor and helps use up those small amounts of food.

Prep Time: 10 Minutes | **Start to Finish:** 35 Minutes | 6 servings

1 tablespoon butter or margarine

1 small bell pepper (any color), chopped (½ cup)

1 small onion, chopped (¼ cup)

12 eggs

1 container (8 oz) sour cream

½ teaspoon salt

⅛ teaspoon pepper

1½ cups shredded Cheddar-Monterey Jack cheese blend (6 oz)

$1.24 *per serving*

1 Heat oven to 325°F. Spray 12×8-inch (2-quart) glass baking dish with cooking spray. In 8-inch skillet, melt butter over medium heat. Add bell pepper and onion; cook 2 to 3 minutes, stirring occasionally, until tender.

2 In large bowl, beat eggs, sour cream, salt and pepper with whisk until well blended. Stir in bell pepper mixture and cheese. Pour into baking dish.

3 Bake uncovered 20 to 25 minutes or until eggs are set. Cut into squares to serve. Garnish with parsley, if desired.

1 Serving: Calories 360; Total Fat 29g (Saturated Fat 14g; Trans Fat 0.5g); Cholesterol 480mg; Sodium 510mg; Total Carbohydrate 4g (Dietary Fiber 0g) **Exchanges:** 3 Medium-Fat Meat, 3 Fat **Carbohydrate Choices:** 0

$mart $avings

Add a bit of spice to this recipe with Colby-Monterey Jack cheese with jalapeño peppers instead of the Cheddar-Monterey Jack cheese blend.

Artichoke-Spinach Strata

Strata, an egg dish made with bread, makes a great dinner dish because it can be prepared ahead, baked in one dish, and packed with a variety of vegetables and cheeses.

Prep Time: 20 Minutes | **Start to Finish:** 5 Hours 30 Minutes | 8 servings

2 teaspoons olive or vegetable oil

1 medium bell pepper (any color), finely chopped (1 cup)

1 medium onion, finely chopped (½ cup)

2 cloves garlic, finely chopped

1 can (14 oz) quartered artichoke hearts, drained, coarsely chopped (1½ cups)

1 box (9 oz) frozen spinach, thawed, squeezed to drain

8 cups cubed (1 inch) rustic round bread (about 1 lb)

1½ cups shredded Monterey Jack cheese (6 oz)

6 eggs

2½ cups milk

½ teaspoon ground mustard

1 teaspoon salt

¼ teaspoon pepper

½ cup shredded Parmesan cheese (2 oz)

$**1.81** *per serving*

1 In 10-inch nonstick skillet, heat oil over medium heat. Add bell pepper, onion and garlic; cook about 6 minutes, stirring occasionally, until tender. Remove from heat. Stir in artichokes and spinach; set aside.

2 Spray 13×9-inch (3-quart) glass baking dish with cooking spray. Arrange bread cubes in dish. Spoon vegetable mixture evenly over bread cubes; sprinkle with Monterey Jack cheese.

3 In medium bowl, beat eggs, milk, mustard, salt and pepper with whisk until blended; pour evenly over bread, vegetables and cheese. Sprinkle with Parmesan cheese. Cover tightly with foil; refrigerate at least 4 hours but no longer than 24 hours.

4 Heat oven to 350°F. Bake covered 30 minutes. Uncover; bake 20 to 30 minutes longer or until top is golden brown and knife inserted in center comes out clean. Let stand 10 minutes before cutting.

1 Serving: Calories 390; Total Fat 17g (Saturated Fat 8g; Trans Fat 0.5g); Cholesterol 190mg; Sodium 980mg; Total Carbohydrate 35g (Dietary Fiber 7g) **Exchanges:** 1 Starch, 1 Other Carbohydrate, 1 Vegetable, 2½ Medium-Fat Meat, 1 Fat **Carbohydrate Choices:** 2

$mart $avings

As those ends of bread become too stale to enjoy, put them in a freezer container, and freeze to use for strata. It doesn't matter if it is a variety of breads because all the flavors and textures will blend together as it soaks in the egg mixture. You can use any shredded cheese you have on hand, such as mozzarella, Swiss or Cheddar.

Scrambled Egg Burritos

Burritos can be filled with various mixtures, but we have taken a breakfast favorite, scrambled eggs, to make an inexpensive and quick dinner dish.

Prep Time: 15 Minutes | **Start to Finish:** 15 Minutes | 4 burritos

1 medium bell pepper (any color), chopped (1 cup)

1 large onion, chopped (1 cup)

6 eggs

2 egg whites

1/3 cup fat-free (skim) milk

1/2 teaspoon salt

1/8 teaspoon pepper

4 fat-free flour tortillas (10 inch)

1/2 cup shredded nonfat Cheddar cheese (2 oz)

1/4 cup chunky-style salsa

$**1.55** per serving

1 Spray 12-inch nonstick skillet with cooking spray. Heat over medium heat until hot. Add bell pepper and onion; cover and cook 4 to 6 minutes or until tender.

2 In medium bowl, beat eggs, egg whites, milk, salt and pepper with whisk. Pour egg mixture into skillet. As mixture begins to set at bottom and side, gently lift cooked portions with turner so that thin, uncooked portion can flow to bottom. Avoid constant stirring. Cook 3 to 4 minutes or until egg mixture is thickened throughout but still moist.

3 Meanwhile, heat tortillas as directed on package. Place tortillas on 4 individual plates. Spoon scrambled egg mixture down center of each tortilla. Top each with cheese and salsa; roll up.

1 Burrito: Calories 360; Total Fat 17g (Saturated Fat 6g; Trans Fat 0.5g); Cholesterol 335mg; Sodium 920mg; Total Carbohydrate 33g (Dietary Fiber 2g) **Exchanges:** 2 Starch, 2 Medium-Fat Meat, 1 Fat **Carbohydrate Choices:** 2

$mart $avings

Calories and fat are reduced by using fat-free ingredients, but you can make this easy dish by using 7 whole eggs, regular flour tortillas and regular cheese along with whatever milk you have in the refrigerator.

Vegetable Frittata

This frittata, an Italian egg dish, becomes a one-dish meal when it is packed with fresh vegetables. Serve with your favorite fresh fruit.

Prep Time: 20 Minutes | **Start to Finish:** 45 Minutes | 8 servings

6 eggs

2 tablespoons milk

1/3 cup shredded Parmesan cheese

1/8 teaspoon garlic powder

1/2 teaspoon dried basil leaves

1/4 teaspoon salt

1/4 teaspoon pepper

6 medium green onions, sliced (6 tablespoons)

2 teaspoons olive or vegetable oil

2 small unpeeled red potatoes, cubed (1 cup)

6 oz fresh spinach, stems removed, leaves torn into bite-size pieces (about 6 cups loosely packed)

5 cherry tomatoes, quartered

$0.58 *per serving*

1   In medium bowl, beat eggs and milk with whisk. Stir in cheese, garlic powder, basil, salt, pepper and onions.

2   In 9- to 10-inch nonstick skillet with sloping sides (omelet or crepe pan), heat oil over medium heat. Cook potatoes in oil about 5 minutes, stirring frequently, until tender. Add spinach; cover and cook 1 to 2 minutes or until spinach is wilted.

3   Reduce heat to low. Spread potatoes and spinach evenly in skillet; top evenly with tomatoes. Pour egg mixture over top. Cover; cook 12 to 15 minutes, lifting edges occasionally to allow uncooked egg mixture to flow to bottom of skillet, until bottom is lightly browned and top is set. Cut into wedges.

1 Serving: Calories 110; Total Fat 7g (Saturated Fat 2g; Trans Fat 0g); Cholesterol 165mg; Sodium 220mg; Total Carbohydrate 6g (Dietary Fiber 1g) **Exchanges:** 1 Vegetable, 1 Medium-Fat Meat, 1/2 Fat **Carbohydrate Choices:** 1/2

$mart $avings

You can use a small tomato, seeded and chopped, for the cherry tomatoes, and a small chopped onion (1/4 cup) for the green onions. Want to add an extra vegetable? Add some chopped bell pepper, zucchini slices or a shredded carrot.

Cheese- and Vegetable-Stuffed Shells

Stuffed pasta shells make a hearty main dish and are a great way to slip a few extra veggies into the family diet without them even noticing.

Prep Time: 40 Minutes | **Start to Finish:** 1 Hour 20 Minutes | 4 servings

16 uncooked jumbo pasta shells

1 tablespoon olive or vegetable oil

1 medium onion, chopped ($^1/_2$ cup)

1 small bell pepper (any color), chopped ($^1/_2$ cup)

2 cloves garlic, finely chopped

1 small zucchini, diced (about $^3/_4$ cup)

1 can (2 $^1/_4$ oz) sliced ripe olives, drained

1 jar (14 to 15 oz) tomato pasta sauce

$^1/_2$ cup ricotta cheese

1 egg

1 cup shredded Italian cheese blend or mozzarella cheese (4 oz)

$^1/_4$ cup grated Parmesan cheese

$2.62 *per serving*

1 Heat oven to 350°F. Spray 11×7-inch (2-quart) glass baking dish with cooking spray. Cook and drain pasta shells as directed on package.

2 Meanwhile, in 10-inch skillet, heat oil over medium heat until hot. Cook onion, bell pepper and garlic in oil 2 to 3 minutes, stirring occasionally, until crisp-tender. Add zucchini; cook 4 minutes, stirring occasionally.

3 Stir in olives and $^1/_4$ cup of the pasta sauce. Cook, stirring frequently, until hot. Remove from heat.

4 In medium bowl, mix ricotta cheese, egg, Parmesan cheese and $^1/_2$ cup of the shredded cheese blend. Stir in zucchini mixture until well mixed.

5 Fill each cooked pasta shell with about 2 tablespoons zucchini mixture. Place in baking dish. Pour remaining pasta sauce over shells.

6 Cover with foil; bake 30 minutes. Sprinkle with remaining $^1/_2$ cup shredded cheese. Bake uncovered 5 to 10 minutes longer or until bubbly and cheese is melted.

1 Serving (4 shells): Calories 510; Total Fat 22g (Saturated Fat 9g; Trans Fat 0g); Cholesterol 85mg; Sodium 1160mg; Total Carbohydrate 55g (Dietary Fiber 4g) **Exchanges:** 2 Starch, 1 $^1/_2$ Other Carbohydrate, 1 Vegetable, 2 High-Fat Meat, 1 Fat **Carbohydrate Choices:** 3$^1/_2$

$mart $avings

Prefer to make tomato pasta sauce rather than purchase a jar? Use 3 cups of your favorite pasta sauce recipe. If you have a 1-pound bag of frozen bell pepper and onion stir-fry vegetables in the freezer, use 1 cup of the mixture for the $^1/_2$ cup bell pepper and onion. It will save a little time chopping the pepper and onion.

No One Will Miss the Meat

Garden Vegetable Lasagna

No one will miss the Italian sausage in this lasagna because it's packed with good-for-you vegetables.

Prep Time: 50 Minutes | **Start to Finish:** 1 Hour 55 Minutes | 8 servings

8	uncooked lasagna noodles
1	tablespoon olive or vegetable oil
1	clove garlic, finely chopped
3	cups frozen broccoli cuts
1 ½	cups sliced fresh mushrooms (about 4 oz)
1	medium bell pepper (any color), coarsely chopped (about 1 cup)
1	egg
1	container (15 oz) ricotta cheese
1	teaspoon Italian seasoning
1	jar (26 to 28 oz) chunky vegetable tomato pasta sauce
2	cups shredded Italian cheese blend (8 oz)

$1.81 *per serving*

1 Cook lasagna noodles as directed on package. Drain; place in cold water to cool.

2 Meanwhile, heat oven to 350°F. In 10-inch skillet, heat oil over medium-high heat until hot. Add garlic, broccoli, mushrooms and bell pepper; cook 3 to 4 minutes, stirring frequently, until vegetables are crisp-tender. Remove from heat. If necessary, cut broccoli into smaller pieces.

3 In small bowl, beat egg with whisk. Add ricotta cheese and Italian seasoning; mix well.

4 Drain cooled lasagna noodles. In ungreased 13×9-inch (3-quart) glass baking dish, spread ½ cup of the pasta sauce. Top with 4 noodles, overlapping as necessary, half of ricotta mixture, half of cooked vegetables, half of remaining pasta sauce (about 2 ¼ cups) and 1 cup of the shredded cheese. Repeat layers, starting with noodles.

5 Bake 45 to 50 minutes or until hot and bubbly. If cheese is getting too brown, cover baking dish loosely with foil. Let stand 15 minutes before serving.

1 Serving: Calories 410; Total Fat 18g (Saturated Fat 9g; Trans Fat 0g); Cholesterol 65mg; Sodium 780mg; Total Carbohydrate 41g (Dietary Fiber 4g) **Exchanges:** 1 ½ Starch, 1 Other Carbohydrate, 1 Vegetable, 2 High-Fat Meat **Carbohydrate Choices:** 3

$mart $avings

Use another combination of Italian cheeses from your refrigerator in place of the Italian blend. Try Asiago, mozzarella, Parmesan and provolone; shred the cheeses, and measure 2 cups. And if you have other odds 'n ends in the refrigerator, you can add them, too—those few roasted bell peppers in the jar, thinly sliced, those couple of green onions—or shred that last lonely carrot.

No-Roll
Mexican Rice
Enchiladas

Enchiladas can be assembled earlier in the day and refrigerated with the sauce. Pour the enchilada sauce over the enchiladas just before baking. Enchiladas may need to bake 5 to 10 minutes longer.

Prep Time: 30 Minutes | **Start to Finish:** 1 Hour 5 Minutes | 5 servings

1   box (6.4 oz) rice and vermicelli mix with Spanish seasonings

2   tablespoons butter or margarine

2 ¼   cups water

1   can (19 oz) mild enchilada sauce

1   can (16 oz) pinto beans, drained, rinsed

1   can (11 oz) southwestern style corn, drained

10   flour tortillas (6 to 8-inch)

2   cups finely shredded Mexican cheese blend (8 oz)

$2.13 *per serving*

1 Spray 13×9-inch (3-quart) glass baking dish with cooking spray. In 12-inch nonstick skillet, cook rice and vermicelli mix with butter over medium heat until rice mixture is golden brown, stirring frequently. Stir in water and seasoning mix from rice box. Heat to boiling. Cover; reduce heat to low. Cook 15 to 20 minutes or until rice mixture is tender. Stir in ½ cup of the enchilada sauce, the pinto beans and corn.

2 Heat oven to 350°F. Place about ½ cup rice mixture on center of each tortilla; top rice mixture in each tortilla with about 1 tablespoon of the cheese. Fold each in half. Arrange tortillas in 2 rows of 5 in baking dish, placing tortillas open end up, slanting and overlapping. Pour remaining enchilada sauce evenly over enchiladas. Cover tightly with foil.

3 Bake 30 to 35 minutes or until hot and sauce begins to bubble. Uncover; sprinkle with remaining cheese. Bake uncovered about 5 minutes longer or until cheese is melted. Garnish as desired.

1 Serving (2 enchiladas): Calories 600; Total Fat 23g (Saturated Fat 11g; Trans Fat 1g); Cholesterol 50mg; Sodium 1420mg; Total Carbohydrate 73g (Dietary Fiber 12g) **Exchanges:** 4 Starch, ½ Low-Fat Milk, ½ Vegetable, 2 Very Lean Meat, 3 Fat **Carbohydrate Choices:** 5

$mart $avings

One can (15.25 ounces) whole kernel sweet corn, drained, can be used instead of the southwestern style corn. One can (15 ounces) black beans, drained and rinsed, can be used in place of the pinto beans.

Lentil-Barley-Vegetable Skillet

This easy skillet meal is full of nutrients but won't empty your wallet.

Prep Time: 15 Minutes | **Start to Finish:** 55 Minutes | 6 servings

1 tablespoon vegetable oil

1 cup dried lentils, sorted, rinsed

1 medium carrot, sliced (½ cup)

1 small onion, coarsely chopped (⅓ cup)

¾ cup uncooked quick-cooking barley

1 teaspoon dried basil leaves

¼ teaspoon pepper

2 cans (14 oz each) vegetable broth

1 medium bell pepper (any color), cut into thin bite-size strips

1 medium stalk celery, sliced (½ cup)

1 cup frozen whole kernel corn

1 can (14.5 oz) diced tomatoes with Italian herbs, undrained

Shredded fresh Parmesan cheese, if desired

$1.49 *per serving*

1 In 12-inch skillet, heat oil over medium heat until hot. Cook lentils, carrot and onion in oil 3 minutes, stirring frequently.

2 Stir in barley, basil, pepper and broth. Heat to boiling. Reduce heat to medium-low; cover and simmer about 20 minutes or until lentils are tender but still firm.

3 Stir in remaining ingredients except cheese. Increase heat to medium; cover and simmer 10 to 15 minutes longer, stirring occasionally, until lentils and vegetables are tender and liquid is almost absorbed. Sprinkle individual servings with Parmesan cheese.

1 Serving: Calories 280; Total Fat 3g (Saturated Fat 0.5g, Trans Fat 0g); Cholesterol 0mg; Sodium 700mg; Total Carbohydrate 50g (Dietary Fiber 11g) **Exchanges:** 2 Starch, 1 Other Carbohydrate, 1 Vegetable, ½ Lean Meat **Carbohydrate Choices:** 3

$mart $avings

You can use a cup of any frozen vegetables that you have on hand, such as cut green beans, broccoli florets, asparagus cuts or sweet peas. A few fresh mushrooms in the refrigerator? Throw those in, too.

Smoky Three-Bean Chili

Chipotle chiles (dried smoked jalapeño chiles) and adobo sauce add a smoky and spicy flavor to this hearty chili packed with inexpensive beans. Serve with your favorite chili toppings, such as chopped onion, shredded cheese and chips.

Prep Time: 50 Minutes | **Start to Finish:** 50 Minutes | 6 servings

1 tablespoon vegetable oil

2 medium stalks celery, chopped (1 cup)

1 medium bell pepper (any color), chopped (1 cup)

1 medium onion, chopped (½ cup)

2 cloves garlic, finely chopped

1 can (28 oz) diced tomatoes, undrained

1 can (15 oz) spicy chili beans, undrained

1 can (15 oz) kidney beans, drained, rinsed

1 can (15 oz) black beans, drained, rinsed

1 teaspoon ground cumin

1 teaspoon chili powder

1 teaspoon finely chopped chipotle chile in adobo sauce (from 7- or 11-oz can)

½ teaspoon adobo sauce (from can of chipotle chiles)

$**1.24** *per serving*

1 In 4-quart Dutch oven or skillet, heat oil over medium-high heat until hot. Add celery, bell pepper, onion and garlic; cook and stir 3 minutes.

2 Add remaining ingredients; mix well. Heat to boiling. Reduce heat; cover and simmer 30 to 40 minutes, stirring occasionally, until vegetables are tender and flavors are blended.

1 Serving: Calories 270; Total Fat 4g (Saturated Fat 0.5g; Trans Fat 0g); Cholesterol 0mg; Sodium 1030mg; Total Carbohydrate 45g (Dietary Fiber 13g) **Exchanges:** 2 Starch, ½ Other Carbohydrate, 1 Vegetable, 1 Lean Meat **Carbohydrate Choices:** 3

$mart $avings

You can increase the chili powder to 2 teaspoons if you don't want to purchase a can of chipotle chiles in adobo sauce. Almost to the end of that bag of tortilla chips? Crush what's left in the bag, and sprinkle on top of each serving of chili. Slice a green onion or two to sprinkle on and serve with that container of sour cream tucked in the back of the refrigerator.

Chick Pea and Tomato Curry

This flavorful curried chick pea dish can be served in a bowl. Or, to make it a heartier meal, serve over hot basmati rice, and top with a dollop of plain yogurt.

Prep Time: 30 Minutes | **Start to Finish:** 30 Minutes | 6 servings

1 tablespoon olive or vegetable oil

1 medium onion, chopped (½ cup)

3 cloves garlic, finely chopped

1 tablespoon finely chopped gingerroot

1 tablespoon curry powder

2 cans (15 oz each) chick peas or garbanzo beans, drained, rinsed

2 cans (14.5 oz each) diced tomatoes, undrained

½ cup finely chopped fresh cilantro

1 tablespoon fresh lemon juice

½ teaspoon salt

Hot cooked rice, if desired

Plain yogurt, if desired

$0.97 *per serving*

1 In 3-quart saucepan, heat oil over medium heat. Cook onion, garlic, gingerroot and curry powder in oil about 2 minutes, stirring frequently, until onion is tender.

2 Stir in chick peas and tomatoes. Heat to boiling. Reduce heat; simmer uncovered 15 minutes, stirring occasionally. Stir in cilantro, lemon juice and salt.

3 Serve over rice; serve with yogurt.

1 Serving (1 cup): Calories 270; Total Fat 6g (Saturated Fat 0.5g; Trans Fat 0g); Cholesterol 0mg; Sodium 380mg; Total Carbohydrate 42g (Dietary Fiber 10g) **Exchanges:** 2 Starch, ½ Other Carbohydrate, 1 Vegetable, ½ Very Lean Meat, 1 Fat **Carbohydrate Choices:** 3

$mart $avings

Cilantro complements the curry flavor in this dish. Look for cilantro that is very green, fresh looking and aromatic. To store, snip off the ends of the stems and place in a glass in about 1 inch of water. Seal the glass in a resealable food-storage plastic bag, and it will keep up to a week or longer.

Double Cheese and Bean Nachos

Cheesy nachos, an appetizer favorite, make an inexpensive quick dinner. And to make it even quicker, layer the nachos on a microwavable plate; microwave uncovered on Medium 2 to 4 minutes or until the cheese is melted.

Prep Time: 10 Minutes | **Start to Finish:** 25 Minutes | 8 servings

- 4 cups small round corn tortilla chips
- 1 cup refried beans (from 16-oz can)
- ½ cup chunky-style salsa
- 2 tablespoons pickled jalapeño slices, drained, chopped (from 12-oz jar)
- 8 medium green onions, chopped (½ cup)
- 2 cups shredded Mexican cheese blend (8 oz)

$0.75 *per serving*

1 Heat oven to 400°F. Line 12-inch pizza pan or 15×10×1-inch pan with foil; spray with cooking spray. Spread half of chips evenly on pan.

2 In small bowl, mix refried beans and salsa. Drop about half of mixture by small spoonfuls over chips. Top with half each of jalapeño slices, green onions and cheese. Repeat layers ending with cheese.

3 Bake 10 to 12 minutes or until cheese is melted. Serve immediately.

1 Serving: Calories 220; Total Fat 13g (Saturated Fat 6g; Trans Fat 0g); Cholesterol 30mg; Sodium 450mg; Total Carbohydrate 17g (Dietary Fiber 2g) **Exchanges:** 1 Starch, 1 High-Fat Meat, 1 Fat **Carbohydrate Choices:** 1

$mart $avings

You can use a couple of fresh chopped jalapeño chiles if you don't have a jar of pickled jalapeños. Just remember to handle the chiles carefully, and don't touch your face or eyes—or to be on the safe side, wear plastic or rubber gloves to protect your hands.

Asian Vegetable Stir-Fry

These stir-fry veggies make a great side to any meat entrée by just omitting the rice.

Prep Time: 25 Minutes | **Start to Finish:** 25 Minutes | 4 servings

1 tablespoon olive oil

1 medium onion, chopped (½ cup)

1 medium carrot, sliced (½ cup)

2 cloves garlic, finely chopped

2 cups uncooked instant white rice

2 cups water

8 oz fresh mushrooms, sliced (3 cups)

1 bag (12 oz) frozen broccoli, water chestnuts, red pepper strips and orange sesame sauce

½ cup stir-fry sauce

⅛ teaspoon red pepper flakes

$2.09 *per serving*

1 In 12-inch skillet, heat oil over medium heat. Cook onion, carrot and garlic in oil 5 to 7 minutes, stirring occasionally, until slightly tender.

2 Cook rice in water as directed on package; cover to keep warm.

3 Into mixture in skillet, stir mushrooms, frozen vegetables in sauce, stir-fry sauce and pepper flakes; cook 5 to 7 minutes, stirring occasionally, until vegetables are tender. Serve over rice.

1 Serving: Calories 330; Total Fat 6g (Saturated Fat 1g, Trans Fat 0g); Cholesterol 0mg; Sodium 1160mg; Total Carbohydrate 62g (Dietary Fiber 4g) **Exchanges:** 2 Starch, 2 Other Carbohydrate, 1 Vegetable, ½ Fat **Carbohydrate Choices:** 4

$mart $avings

This is a good recipe for using up any leftover vegetables you have in your refrigerator, such as celery, broccoli or bell pepper. Just cut them up and add with the onion and carrot.

Crescent-Topped Ratatouille Casserole

Fill your basket with the fresh veggies at the farmers' market to make this heartier variation of ratatouille. Ratatouille originated in the Provence region of France and is a combination of eggplant, bell pepper, zucchini and tomatoes.

Prep Time: 25 Minutes | **Start to Finish:** 1 Hour 10 Minutes | 6 servings

- 1 tablespoon olive or vegetable oil
- 1 small eggplant (1 ¼ lb), cut into ¾-inch cubes (4 cups)
- 1 medium zucchini, sliced
- 1 medium onion, sliced
- 1 medium green bell pepper, cut into 1-inch pieces
- 1 clove garlic, finely chopped
- 1 can (14.5 oz) diced tomatoes, undrained
- 1 can (8 oz) tomato sauce
- ½ teaspoon dried basil leaves
- ¼ teaspoon Italian seasoning
- ⅛ teaspoon coarse ground black pepper
- 1 can (15.5 oz) dark red kidney beans, drained, rinsed
- 1 can (8 oz) refrigerated crescent dinner rolls or refrigerated seamless flaky dough sheet
- 2 tablespoons grated Parmesan cheese
- Chopped parsley, if desired

$2.77 *per serving*

1 In 10-inch skillet, heat oil over medium-high heat until hot. Add eggplant, zucchini, onion, bell pepper and garlic; cook and stir 4 to 6 minutes or until vegetables are lightly browned.

2 Reduce heat to medium-low. Stir in tomatoes, tomato sauce, basil, Italian seasoning and pepper. Cover; simmer about 10 minutes or until vegetables are crisp-tender. Stir in beans; cook 5 minutes longer.

3 Meanwhile, remove dough from can; do not unroll dough. Cut into 8 slices; cut each slice into quarters. Place cheese in 1-quart resealable food-storage plastic bag; add dough pieces, seal bag and shake to coat.

4 Heat oven to 375°F. Spray 11×8-inch (2-quart) glass baking dish with cooking spray. Spoon eggplant mixture into baking dish. Arrange dough pieces on top.

5 Bake 17 to 20 minutes or until dough is golden brown. Sprinkle with chopped parsley.

1 Serving: Calories 320; Total Fat 12g (Saturated Fat 3.5g; Trans Fat 2g); Cholesterol 0mg; Sodium 620mg; Total Carbohydrate 43g (Dietary Fiber 8g) **Exchanges:** 1 ½ Starch, ½ Other Carbohydrate, 3 Vegetable, 2 Fat **Carbohydrate Choices:** 3

$mart $avings

A can of kidney beans and topping of crescent dinner rolls is an inexpensive way to stretch this healthy vegetable dish. And to save time on a busy day, make the eggplant mixture a day ahead, cover and refrigerate. Heat the ratatouille in the oven or microwave until bubbly; top with the dough pieces and bake as directed.

Edamame Corn Chowder

Edamame, the "new" lima bean, is another name for green soybeans, which are an economical source of protein.

Prep Time: 40 Minutes | **Start to Finish:** 40 Minutes | 6 servings

1 tablespoon canola oil

1 medium onion, chopped (1/2 cup)

1 bag (12 oz) frozen shelled edamame (green) soybeans

2 tablespoons all-purpose flour

3/4 teaspoon salt

1/4 teaspoon pepper

4 cups milk

1 can (14.75 oz) cream style sweet corn

1 can (11 oz) whole kernel sweet corn

4 cups frozen southern-style diced hash brown potatoes (from 32-oz bag), thawed

1/4 cup chopped green or red bell pepper, if desired

Chopped fresh parsley, if desired

$**1.52** *per serving*

1 In 4-quart saucepan, heat in oil over medium-high heat. Cook onion in oil, stirring frequently, about 2 minutes or until tender.

2 Using whisk, stir flour, salt and pepper into onion mixture. Cook over medium-high heat, stirring constantly. Stir in milk. Heat to boiling, stirring constantly. Boil and stir 1 minute.

3 Stir edamame, both cans corn and potatoes into milk mixture. Heat to boiling. Reduce heat to low; cover and simmer 10 to 15 minutes or until potatoes are tender. Stir in bell pepper. Top each serving with parsley.

1 Serving (1 1/3 cups): Calories 350; Total Fat 9g (Saturated Fat 2.5g, Trans Fat 0g); Cholesterol 15mg; Sodium 720mg; Total Carbohydrate 52g (Dietary Fiber 6g) **Exchanges:** 2 1/2 Starch, 1/2 Low-Fat Milk, 2 Vegetable, 1 Fat **Carbohydrate Choices:** 3 1/2

$mart $avings

You can easily add some bacon to this rich chowder. Just omit the oil and cook the bacon. Then use the drippings to cook the onion. Stir the crumbled bacon into the chowder with the potatoes.

Chunky Tomato-Basil Soup

That favorite tomato soup you had at the cozy cafe? Easy—start with chunky tomato pasta sauce, some half-and-half, and top it off with plenty of fresh basil. That's it!

Prep Time: 30 Minutes | **Start to Finish:** 30 Minutes | 4 servings

- 2 tablespoons butter or margarine
- 1 medium onion, chopped (½ cup)
- 3 small carrots, shredded (1 cup)
- 2 tablespoons all-purpose flour
- 1 cup half-and-half or fat-free half-and-half
- 1 jar (26 oz) chunky tomato pasta sauce
- 1 can (14.5 oz) diced tomatoes, undrained
- ¼ cup chopped fresh basil leaves, if desired

$1.51 *per serving*

1 In 3-quart saucepan, heat butter over medium-high heat. Add onion and carrots; cook and stir 3 to 4 minutes or until softened. Add flour; cook and stir until moistened. Gradually add half-and-half, cooking and stirring about 2 minutes or until smooth.

2 Stir in remaining ingredients. Cover; cook over medium heat about 15 minutes, stirring frequently, just until mixture comes to a boil. Top with additional chopped fresh basil leaves.

1 Serving (1 ¼ cups each): Calories 400; Total Fat 19g (Saturated Fat 9g, Trans Fat 0g); Cholesterol 40mg; Sodium 1140mg; Total Carbohydrate 50g (Dietary Fiber 5g) **Exchanges:** 1 Starch, 2 Other Carbohydrate, 1 ½ Vegetable, 3½ Fat **Carbohydrate Choices:** 3

$mart $avings

Enjoy variety at no extra cost by using diced tomatoes with different seasonings. If you are a garlic lover, use diced tomatoes with roasted garlic for a little more punch. Or try diced tomatoes with mild green chiles and top with chopped cilantro rather than basil.

Onion-Mushroom Soup with Cheesy Rounds

This is a variation of French onion soup, which is typically topped with a slice of French bread and lots of Swiss cheese and then broiled. This recipe replaces the French bread with cheese rounds made from refrigerated crescent dough, which are great for dunking, too.

Prep Time: 50 Minutes | **Start to Finish:** 1 Hour 5 Minutes | 4 servings

- 2 tablespoons butter or margarine
- 1 tablespoon vegetable oil
- 5 medium onions, thinly sliced (about 5 cups)
- 1 teaspoon packed brown sugar
- 2 cups sliced fresh mushrooms (about 5 oz)
- 2 teaspoons all-purpose flour
- 1 teaspoon salt
- 3 ½ cups vegetable or beef-flavored broth (from 32-oz carton)
- 2 ½ cups water
- 1 can (8 oz) refrigerated crescent dinner rolls or refrigerated seamless flaky dough sheet
- 2 tablespoons grated Parmesan cheese
- ½ teaspoon dried thyme leaves
- ½ cup finely shredded Swiss cheese (2 oz)

$2.33 *per serving*

1 In 4-quart Dutch oven or saucepan, heat butter and oil over medium heat until butter is melted. Add onions; cook about 15 minutes, stirring frequently, until onions are tender and light golden brown.

2 Stir in brown sugar. Cook about 5 minutes, stirring occasionally, until golden brown. Add mushrooms; cook about 5 minutes, stirring occasionally, until tender. Stir in flour and salt. Stir in broth and water. Heat to boiling. Reduce heat. Cover; simmer 20 minutes.

3 Meanwhile, heat oven to 375°F. On ungreased cookie sheet, unroll dough into 1 large rectangle; if using crescent roll dough, press perforations to seal. Sprinkle Parmesan cheese and thyme evenly over dough. Starting with 1 short side, roll up. Cut roll into 8 slices; place cut sides down on cookie sheet. Press slices to form 3-inch rounds.

4 Bake 10 to 14 minutes or until golden brown. Sprinkle each with Swiss cheese. Bake 1 to 2 minutes longer or until cheese is melted and begins to brown.

5 Ladle soup into individual soup bowls. Top each with 1 cheese round. Serve soup with additional cheese rounds.

1 Serving (2 cups soup and 2 rounds): Calories 450; Total Fat 27g (Saturated Fat 12g; Trans Fat 3.5g); Cholesterol 30mg; Sodium 2060mg; Total Carbohydrate 39g (Dietary Fiber 3g) **Exchanges:** 2 Starch, 1 Vegetable, 1 Medium-Fat Meat, 4 Fat **Carbohydrate Choices:** 2 ½

$mart $avings

Mushrooms have been added to this French onion soup to make it a heartier dish. You can add other vegetables if you like, such as a shredded carrot or some chopped celery, when you cook the onion.

CHAPTER 5

Snacks To Go or Eat at Home

It's the little things that count. The handwritten note tucked into a lunch box. A flower plucked from the backyard in a vase on the windowsill. The homemade snacks, ready when stomachs growl, that save you from feeding the vending machine another dollar. The same is true in the kitchen.

Prep for Success

Whipping up delicious, inexpensive snacks is only half the battle. Making sure they're easy to eat, both at home and on the fly, ensures that your budget cooking and purchasing skills don't go to waste.

Portion Break down big-batch snacks into smaller servings, such as shared servings to eat during movie night or single servings to take on the go. Resealable food-storage plastic bags work well, but so do re-purposed plastic food containers—and they're crush-proof.

Cut Dips and spreads always move faster when the fresh veggies and fruit that go with them are cut up and ready. Plus, doing all your chopping at once saves time. Tip: Coat cut-up apples and pears with a little citrus juice to keep them fresh longer.

Tempt Always put what you want your family to eat within easy reach. Keep bowls full of fruit, party mix or energy bars on the counter. Place refrigerated snacks front and center, or at kid-height eye level.

Carry Head off budget-busting last-resort conve-nience store and vending machine purchases. Stash durable snacks in the car, your desk drawer, your purse, or your child's backpack. Don't leave home without them!

Convenience Costs

Keep in mind that the more work done for you—extra packaging or chopping, for example—the more you pay. Do you have the time to shred your own cheese, tear a head of iceberg lettuce into bite-size pieces, mix your own lemonade and create your own snacks?

Not Just a Pre-Meal Snack Anymore

Sure, appetizers are a great way to work up to dinner, but they're delicious—and often money-saving—in many other settings as well.

Social Meal Eating appetizers as a meal is a fine way to encourage conversation and eat a variety of foods in one sitting. It's a cost-effective way to dine out, but you can do it at home, too—it's easiest with leftovers. Just set out a few small plates of food, rather than a main course and many sides.

Easy Party Potluck parties are back, but they look different than when your parents threw them. Try appetizers only. Everyone brings a favorite. Lots of

little, portable bites make for a laid-back way to relax, munch and mingle.

Light Lunch A couple of appetizers can stand alone as lunch. If they don't feel substantial enough, pair them with a side salad or a cup of soup.

Snack Time Think of appetizers as bulk treats your family can enjoy at any time. Bake a batch of some-thing the whole family loves to have on hand for easy after-school or after-work snacks.

Party Snack Mix

A party isn't a party without snacks, and this cereal snack will keep the party going for hours. Or, keep individual bags or containers available to grab for a quick snack.

Prep Time: 10 Minutes | **Start to Finish:** 1 Hour 10 Minutes | 24 servings

4	cups Corn Chex® cereal
2	cups Wheat Chex® cereal
2	cups small pretzel sticks
2	cups Spanish peanuts or mixed nuts
¹/₂	cup butter or margarine, melted
1	tablespoon Worcestershire sauce
¹/₈	teaspoon red pepper sauce
1	teaspoon salt
¹/₄	teaspoon garlic powder

$0.19 *per serving*

1 Heat oven to 325°F. In large bowl, mix cereals, pretzel sticks and peanuts.

2 In small bowl, mix butter, Worcestershire sauce, pepper sauce, salt and garlic powder. Pour over cereal mixture; toss to coat. Spread in ungreased 15×10×1-inch pan.

3 Bake 25 to 30 minutes or until lightly toasted, stirring occasionally. Cool 30 minutes. Store in tightly covered container.

1 Serving (¹/₂ cup): Calories 160; Total Fat 10g (Saturated Fat 3.5g; Trans Fat 0g); Cholesterol 10mg; Sodium 320mg; Total Carbohydrate 12g (Dietary Fiber 2g) **Exchanges:** 1 Starch, 2 Fat **Carbohydrate Choices:** 1

$mart $avings

Cereal and pretzel sticks make this snack better for you than a bag of chips. And nuts contain "good fat," so try other nuts, such as whole almonds, walnut pieces or cashews, for the peanuts. Watch for good nut prices at warehouse stores or bulk dispensers.

Chex® Muddy Buddies®

This easy-to-make cereal snack is not only easy on the wallet, but it's better for you than some other treats. The chocolate will satisfy your sweet tooth!

Prep Time: 15 Minutes | **Start to Finish:** 15 Minutes | 18 servings

9 cups Corn Chex®, Rice Chex®, Wheat Chex® or Chocolate Chex® cereal (or combination)

1 cup semisweet chocolate chips

½ cup peanut butter

¼ cup butter or margarine

1 teaspoon vanilla

1 ½ cups powdered sugar

$0.35 *per serving*

1 Into large bowl, measure cereal; set aside.

2 In 1-quart microwavable bowl, microwave chocolate chips, peanut butter and butter uncovered on High 1 minute; stir. Microwave about 30 seconds longer or until mixture can be stirred smooth. Stir in vanilla. Pour mixture over cereal, stirring until evenly coated. Pour into 2-gallon resealable food-storage plastic bag.

3 Add powdered sugar. Seal bag; shake until well coated. Spread on waxed paper to cool. Store in airtight container in refrigerator.

1 Serving (½ cup): Calories 220; Total Fat 9g (Saturated Fat 4g; Trans Fat 0g); Cholesterol 5mg; Sodium 200mg; Total Carbohydrate 30g (Dietary Fiber 1g) **Exchanges:** 1 Starch, 1 Other Carbohydrate, 1 ½ Fat **Carbohydrate Choices:** 2

$mart $avings

Keep a container of these yummy snacks available for the kids to munch on after school. Or, divide the snacks among individual containers so they're ready to pop into a lunch bag or take to nibble on during a sports event. It'll be much cheaper than buying treats at the game.

Banana Nut Energy Bars

Love those energy bars but trying to cut corners? These chewy homemade bars are less expensive than purchased bars.

Prep Time: 20 Minutes | **Start to Finish:** 50 Minutes | 24 bars

4 cups Banana Nut Cheerios® cereal

1 cup sweetened dried cranberries

1/3 cup slivered almonds, toasted*

1/3 cup roasted unsalted sunflower nuts

1/2 cup light corn syrup

1/4 cup packed brown sugar

1/4 cup creamy peanut butter

1 teaspoon vanilla

$0.29 *per serving*

1 Spray 9-inch square pan with cooking spray. In large bowl, mix cereal, cranberries, almonds and sunflower nuts.

2 In 2-quart saucepan, heat corn syrup, brown sugar and peanut butter to boiling over medium-high heat, stirring constantly. Boil and stir 1 minute. Remove from heat; stir in vanilla.

3 Pour syrup mixture over cereal mixture; toss to coat. Press firmly in pan. Cool completely, about 30 minutes. For bars, cut into 6 rows by 4 rows.

1 Bar: Calories 110; Total Fat 3.5g (Saturated Fat 0g; Trans Fat 0g); Cholesterol 0mg; Sodium 55mg; Total Carbohydrate 18g (Dietary Fiber 1g) **Exchanges:** 1/2 Starch, 1/2 Other Carbohydrate, 1/2 Fat **Carbohydrate Choices:** 1

*To toast almonds, heat oven to 350°F. Spread almonds in ungreased shallow pan. Bake uncovered 6 to 10 minutes, stirring occasionally, until light golden brown.

$mart $avings

These are great for tide-me-overs between meals because they're filling and satisfying. Keep a few plastic-wrapped bars in your workout bag or desk drawer. Be creative and use different dried fruits, such as cherries or blueberries, and any nuts you have on hand. And chunky peanut butter works good, too.

Melon-Raspberry Smoothies

No need to purchase expensive health drinks when you can whip up a smoothie with the help of a container of yogurt, a few pieces of fruit and a blender.

Prep Time: 5 Minutes | **Start to Finish:** 5 Minutes | 2 smoothies

1   cup cubed cantaloupe or honeydew melon

1   cup frozen or fresh raspberries

1   container (6 oz) strawberry mango original low-fat yogurt

2   tablespoons milk

1   tablespoon sugar

$2.32 *per serving*

1 In blender or food processor, place all ingredients. Cover; blend on high speed 20 to 30 seconds or until smooth.

2 Pour into 2 glasses. Serve immediately.

1 Smoothie (¾ cup): Calories 180; Total Fat 1.5g (Saturated Fat 0.5g; Trans Fat 0g); Cholesterol 5mg; Sodium 60mg; Total Carbohydrate 37g (Dietary Fiber 4g) **Exchanges:** 1 Starch, 1 Fruit, ½ Other Carbohydrate **Carbohydrate Choices:** 2 ½

Mango-Blueberry Smoothies: Substitute 1 cup cubed mango for the melon and 1 cup fresh or frozen blueberries for the raspberries.

$mart $avings

Look for fresh berries in July and August when they're least expensive. When purchasing fresh berries, make sure to look the package over carefully. The fruit on the bottom shouldn't be bruised, and the fruit should smell sweet, not musty. Store berries unwashed and loosely covered in the refrigerator. Ripe melons give the most flavor, so select ones that are heavy and have a sweet melon aroma.

Strawberry–Key Lime Smoothie

A smoothie is a quick and inexpensive breakfast solution for busy mornings. The combination of fruits and low-fat yogurt makes a flavorful, energy-boosting drink to enjoy any time of the day.

Prep Time: 10 Minutes | **Start to Finish:** 10 Minutes | 1 smoothie

½ medium banana

½ cup frozen strawberries (not in syrup)

½ cup orange juice

1 container (6 oz) Key lime pie original low-fat yogurt

$1.42 *per serving*

1 In blender, place all ingredients. Cover; blend 1 to 2 minutes or until smooth and frothy.

2 Pour into glass; serve immediately.

1 Smoothie (1 ¾ cups): Calories 310; Total Fat 1.5g (Saturated Fat 1g; Trans Fat 0g); Cholesterol 0mg; Sodium 95mg; Total Carbohydrate 66g (Dietary Fiber 4g) **Exchanges:** 3 ½ Fruit, 1 Skim Milk **Carbohydrate Choices:** 4 ½

Strawberry-Berry Smoothie: Substitute 1 container (6 oz) mixed berry original low-fat yogurt for the Key lime pie yogurt.

Strawberry–Double Orange Smoothie: Substitute 1 container (6 oz) orange crème original low-fat yogurt for the Key lime pie yogurt.

Strawberry-Peach Smoothie: Substitute 1 container (6 oz) harvest peach original low-fat yogurt for the Key lime pie yogurt.

$mart $avings

Stock up on yogurt when it's on sale so you can enjoy this smoothie often. Yogurt provides calcium, and if you want to boost your calcium intake, spend a few more cents and use calcium-fortified orange juice. Those frozen ripe bananas in the freezer also work good in smoothies.

Peach-Berry Smoothies

Serve this quick fruit smoothie as an energizing breakfast to jump-start the day or as an after-school snack to welcome the kids home.

Prep Time: 5 Minutes | **Start to Finish:** 5 Minutes | 4 smoothies

2   containers (6 oz each) strawberry original low-fat yogurt

1   cup sliced fresh or frozen peaches or nectarines

1   cup sliced fresh or whole frozen, slightly thawed, strawberries

1   cup crushed ice

$**1.62** *per serving*

1   In blender, place all ingredients. Cover; blend on high speed 30 to 60 seconds or until smooth.

2   Pour into 4 glasses. Serve immediately.

1 Smoothie (1 cup): Calories 120; Total Fat 1g (Saturated Fat 0.5g; Trans Fat 0g); Cholesterol 5mg; Sodium 40mg; Total Carbohydrate 24g (Dietary Fiber 1g) **Exchanges:** 1 Fruit, ½ Skim Milk **Carbohydrate Choices:** 1 ½

$mart $avings

Stock your freezer when bags of frozen fruit and berries are on sale so you can enjoy this drink anytime. No strawberry yogurt? Use whatever flavor yogurt you have on hand—it'll still be tasty and refreshing.

Red Pepper Hummus

For just a few cents, add flavor and color to traditional hummus with the addition of roasted red bell peppers. And make up the cost difference by making your own pita chips.

Prep Time: 10 Minutes | **Start to Finish:** 20 Minutes | 12 servings

3   pita breads (6 inch)

1   can (19 oz) chick peas or garbanzo beans, drained, rinsed

1   tablespoon lemon juice

1   tablespoon olive oil

2   cloves garlic, chopped

⅓   cup drained roasted red bell peppers (from a jar)

Additional olive oil, if desired

Chopped fresh parsley, if desired

$0.52 *per serving*

1   Heat oven to 400°F. Split each pita bread around each edge with knife to make 2 rounds. Cut each round into 8 wedges. On 2 ungreased cookie sheets, place wedges in single layer. Bake about 9 minutes or until crisp and light brown; cool.

2   Meanwhile, in food processor, place chick peas, lemon juice, 1 tablespoon oil and the garlic. Cover; process 1 to 2 minutes or until smooth. Add roasted peppers; process 30 to 60 seconds or until peppers are finely chopped. Place in serving bowl; cover and refrigerate until ready to serve.

3   If desired, make a depression in the middle of the bowl of hummus; spoon in additional olive oil. Sprinkle with parsley. Serve with pita chips. Store any remaining pita chips in airtight container at room temperature.

1 Serving (2 tablespoons hummus and 4 pita chips): Calories 110; Total Fat 2g (Saturated Fat 0g; Trans Fat 0g); Cholesterol 0mg; Sodium 135mg; Total Carbohydrate 17g (Dietary Fiber 2g) **Exchanges:** 1 Starch, ½ Fat **Carbohydrate Choices:** 1

$mart $avings

If you don't have a food processor, mash the chick peas with a fork or potato masher. The mixture may be slightly lumpy, but the texture does not interfere with the flavor. You can omit the roasted red bell peppers and make a more traditional hummus if you like. Add a little more olive oil if the hummus is too thick. Leftover hummus makes a great sandwich spread.

Dilly Veggie Dip

Some of us need a little extra incentive to eat more veggies, but this easy dip is is one your whole family will enjoy. And it costs less than $2.00 to make!

Prep Time: 10 Minutes | **Start to Finish:** 2 Hours 10 Minutes | 12 servings

½ cup light sour cream

¼ cup plain nonfat yogurt

4 medium green onions, chopped (¼ cup)

2 teaspoons dried dill weed or 2 tablespoons chopped fresh dill weed

⅛ teaspoon garlic salt

⅛ teaspoon pepper

Assorted cut-up fresh vegetables, if desired

$0.14 *per serving*

1 In small bowl, mix all ingredients except vegetables. Cover; refrigerate 1 to 2 hours to blend flavors.

2 Stir dip before serving. Serve with vegetables. Cover and refrigerate any remaining dip and vegetables.

1 Serving (2 tablespoons): Calories 35; Total Fat 1g (Saturated Fat 1g; Trans Fat 0g); Cholesterol 10mg; Sodium 50mg; Total Carbohydrate 4g (Dietary Fiber 0g) **Exchanges:** Free **Carbohydrate Choices:** 0

$mart $avings

This is a great way to use all those odds and ends of fresh veggies in the refrigerator. Serving this yummy dip might entice the little ones to eat their veggies, too. It also makes a healthy snack or light lunch to take to work.

Prosciutto and Creamy Blue Cheese Pear Slices

Fruit is always a good choice for a snack or an appetizer. With the addition of salty prosciutto and tangy blue cheese, a simple slice of pear looks and tastes like a million bucks for only pennies.

Prep Time: 10 Minutes | **Start to Finish:** 10 Minutes | 12 snacks

1 oz cream cheese, softened

1 oz crumbled blue cheese (about 3 tablespoons)

1 ripe (not firm) medium pear, cut in half lengthwise, cut into 12 slices

6 thin slices prosciutto, cut in half lengthwise

$**0.23** *per serving*

1 In small bowl, stir cream cheese and blue cheese, using rubber spatula, until well blended.

2 Spread rounded $\frac{1}{2}$ teaspoon cheese mixture on each pear slice. Starting at one end of each pear slice, wrap 1 prosciutto strip in spiral fashion around pear slice.

1 Snack: Calories 40; Total Fat 2g (Saturated Fat 1g; Trans Fat 0g); Cholesterol 10mg; Sodium 150mg; Total Carbohydrate 2g (Dietary Fiber 0g) **Exchanges:** $\frac{1}{2}$ Medium-Fat Meat **Carbohydrate Choices:** 0

Ham and Creamy Blue Cheese Apple Slices: Substitute 6 very thin slices cooked ham for the prosciutto and 1 medium apple, cut into 12 slices, for the pear.

$mart $avings

Prosciutto is an Italian ham that has been seasoned and cured but not smoked, and it's relatively expensive. If you prefer, use thinly sliced cooked ham instead. Pieces of melon also go well with prosciutto and blue cheese, so give it a try.

Banana Boats

Everyone will love these warm, gooey bananas as a snack or dessert—and they're under $0.50 per serving!

Prep Time: 25 Minutes | **Start to Finish:** 45 Minutes | 6 banana boats

6   ripe firm large bananas, unpeeled

6   tablespoons chocolate chips

6   tablespoons miniature marshmallows

2   tablespoons chopped pecans

$0.34 *per serving*

1   Heat oven to 350°F. Cut 6 (12-inch) sheets of heavy-duty foil.

2   With sharp knife, make deep lengthwise cut along inside curve of each banana, being careful not to cut all the way through. Open slit to form pocket. Crimp and shape 1 sheet of foil around each banana, forming boats.

3   Holding each banana in hand, fill pocket with 2 tablespoons chocolate chips, 2 tablespoons marshmallows and about ½ heaping teaspoon chopped pecans.

4   Return each banana to its foil boat. Seal top of foil, leaving 2 to 3 inches headspace. Place foil packets on oven rack; bake 15 to 20 minutes or until marshmallows soften.

1 Banana Boat: Calories 210; Total Fat 5g (Saturated Fat 2g; Trans Fat 0g); Cholesterol 0mg; Sodium 0mg; Total Carbohydrate 39g (Dietary Fiber 4g) **Exchanges:** 2 Fruit, ½ Other Carbohydrate, ½ High-Fat Meat **Carbohydrate Choices:** 2 ½

Grilled Banana Boats: Heat gas or charcoal grill. Place foil-wrapped bananas on grill over medium heat. Cover grill; cook 8 to 10 minutes or until marshmallows soften. (Can also be placed in campfire coals to cook.)

$mart $avings

The banana peel will turn black when heated, but don't worry because they'll still taste wonderful. Watch for bananas on sale to make this a very economical treat.

Ranch Deviled Eggs

No wonder these eggs are called "deviled" because they're devilishly delicious but don't pull any devilish tricks on the budget.

Prep Time: 25 Minutes | **Start to Finish:** 50 Minutes | 12 deviled eggs

6   eggs

3   tablespoons ranch dressing

¹⁄₂   teaspoon yellow mustard

¹⁄₄   cup finely chopped celery

¹⁄₈   teaspoon salt

     Paprika

$0.17 *per serving*

1 In 2-quart saucepan, place eggs in single layer; add enough water to cover eggs by 1 inch. Heat to boiling. Immediately remove from heat; cover and let stand 15 minutes.

2 Drain water from eggs; rinse eggs with cold water. Place eggs in bowl of ice water; let stand 10 minutes.

3 Peel eggs; cut in half lengthwise. Carefully remove yolks; place in small bowl. Mash yolks with fork until smooth. Stir in dressing, mustard, celery and salt until well blended.

4 Spoon yolk mixture into egg white halves. Sprinkle with paprika.

1 Deviled Egg: Calories 60; Total Fat 4.5g (Saturated Fat 1g; Trans Fat 0g); Cholesterol 105mg; Sodium 90mg; Total Carbohydrate 0g (Dietary Fiber 0g) **Exchanges:** ¹⁄₂ Medium-Fat Meat, ¹⁄₂ Fat **Carbohydrate Choices:** 0

$mart $avings

Deviled eggs are great as an appetizer for a casual backyard party. Or keep a container in the fridge for family snacks. Use any creamy dressing or mayonnaise if you don't have ranch dressing on hand.

Turkey Dijon Roll-Ups

Roll-ups are great to have in the fridge for a quick grab-and-eat snack that's better for the family than grabbing a bag of candy or chips.

Prep Time: 20 Minutes | **Start to Finish:** 35 Minutes | 18 roll-ups

2   **tablespoons honey mustard**

3   **herb or plain flour tortillas (8 inch)**

1   **carrot, shredded**

1   **package (6 oz) smoked turkey breast slices**

3   **leaves leaf lettuce**

¼   **cup honey Dijon dressing**

$0.18 *per serving*

1   Spread mustard evenly on tortillas to edges.

2   Top each tortilla evenly with carrot, turkey and lettuce. Roll up each tortilla; wrap securely with plastic wrap. Refrigerate at least 15 minutes but no longer than 12 hours.

3   To serve, cut rolls into ³/₄-inch slices. Serve with dressing.

1 Roll-Up: Calories 45; Total Fat 2g (Saturated Fat 0g; Trans Fat 0g); Cholesterol 0mg; Sodium 190mg; Total Carbohydrate 5g (Dietary Fiber 0g) **Exchanges:** ¹/₂ Starch **Carbohydrate Choices:** ¹/₂

$mart $avings

You can use a package of oven-roasted turkey breast or ham or chicken breast slices if on sale or you have it on hand. Honey mustard adds a nice sweet and hot flavor, but you can use any mustard you have and still enjoy these easy-to-make snacks.

On-the-Go Pepperoni Pizzas

Enjoy pizza any time with English muffins in the pantry and pepperoni mixture in the fridge—and it's more economical than ordering in.

Prep Time: 15 Minutes | **Start to Finish:** 15 Minutes | 6 servings

- 1 **can (8 oz) pizza sauce**
- 1 **package (3 oz) cream cheese, softened**
- 1 **package (8 oz) sliced pepperoni, coarsely chopped (2 ½ cups)**
- 4 **medium green onions, sliced (¼ cup)**
- ¼ **cup finely chopped bell pepper (any color)**
- 1½ **cups shredded mozzarella cheese (6 oz)**
- 6 **English muffins, split, toasted**

$1.72 *per serving*

1 In large bowl, mix pizza sauce and cream cheese until well blended. Stir in pepperoni, onions, bell pepper and 1 cup of the cheese. Cover; serve immediately or refrigerate mixture up to 3 days.

2 To make 1 serving, place 2 toasted muffin halves on microwavable plate. Top each half with about ¼ cup pepperoni mixture and heaping tablespoon remaining cheese. Microwave on High about 1 minute or until hot.

1 Serving (2 pizzas): Calories 470; Total Fat 28g (Saturated Fat 13g; Trans Fat 0g); Cholesterol 60mg; Sodium 1400mg; Total Carbohydrate 33g (Dietary Fiber 2g) **Exchanges:** 1 ½ Starch, ½ Other Carbohydrate, 2 ½ High-Fat Meat, 1 ½ Fat **Carbohydrate Choices:** 2

$mart $avings

You can use bagels, split and toasted, if you don't have English muffins. You can substitute ¼ cup chopped onion for the green onions. Don't care for bell pepper? Leave it out, or try sliced ripe olives instead.

Pizza Dipping Sticks

Mix and match the toppings on these dipping sticks according to your tastes and what you have on hand. Try olives, onions, bell pepper and cooked ground beef or sausage.

Prep Time: 10 Minutes | **Start to Finish:** 35 Minutes | 4 servings

1   can (13.8 oz) refrigerated classic pizza crust

30   slices pepperoni (from 3.5-oz package)

1 ½   cups shredded mozzarella cheese (6 oz)

1   to 1 ½ cups pizza sauce, warmed

$1.65 *per serving*

1 Heat oven to 400°F. Grease or spray cookie sheet. Unroll dough; place on cookie sheet. Starting at center, press out dough into 13×9-inch rectangle.

2 Bake 7 minutes. Top with pepperoni and cheese.

3 Bake 8 to 10 minutes longer or until cheese is melted. Cool 2 minutes. Cut pizza in half lengthwise, then cut into 16 (1 ½-inch) strips. Serve with pizza sauce for dipping.

1 Serving (4 strips): Calories 580; Total Fat 28g (Saturated Fat 13g; Trans Fat 0g); Cholesterol 70mg; Sodium 1940mg; Total Carbohydrate 55g (Dietary Fiber 1g) **Exchanges:** 2 ½ Starch, 1 Other Carbohydrate, 3 High-Fat Meat, ½ Fat **Carbohydrate Choices:** 3 ½

Chile and Cheese Empanaditas

These chile and cheese empanaditas are as easy to prepare as they are easy on the wallet.

Prep Time: 25 Minutes | **Start to Finish:** 45 Minutes | 16 empanaditas

1 cup shredded pepper Jack cheese (4 oz)

⅓ cup chopped green chiles (from 4.5-oz can)

1 box (15 oz) refrigerated pie crusts, softened as directed on box

1 egg, beaten

Sour cream or salsa, if desired

- -

$0.32 *per serving*

1 Heat oven to 400°F. Spray cookie sheet with cooking spray. In small bowl, mix cheese and chiles.

2 With 3 ¼-inch round cutter, cut each pie crust into 8 rounds. Spoon cheese mixture evenly onto half of each dough round. Brush edge of crust rounds with egg. Fold rounds in half; press edges with fork to seal. Place on cookie sheet. Brush tops with egg. Prick top of each round with fork to allow steam to escape.

3 Bake 12 to 16 minutes or until golden brown. Serve warm with sour cream or salsa.

1 Empanadita: Calories 140; Total Fat 9g (Saturated Fat 3.5g; Trans Fat 0g); Cholesterol 25mg; Sodium 170mg; Total Carbohydrate 13g (Dietary Fiber 0g) **Exchanges:** 1 Starch, 1 ½ Fat **Carbohydrate Choices:** 1

Sealing the Edges

$mart $avings

These bite-size snacks can be made ahead, frozen and used for after-school snacks for the kids or for appetizers. After making the foldovers and brushing with egg, freeze them on a cookie sheet until firm. Pop them into a freezer container for up to 2 months. Bake as you need them, and add about 5 minutes to the bake time. Cheddar cheese can be used for the pepper Jack if you have it on hand.

Brown Sugar–Oatmeal Cookies

Need an after-school treat for the kids? These cookies cost only pennies each, and with whole wheat and oatmeal you get two benefits in one—inexpensive and good for them!

Prep Time: 55 Minutes | **Start to Finish:** 55 Minutes | 4 dozen cookies

1 ³/₄ cups packed brown sugar

1 cup butter or margarine, softened

1 teaspoon vanilla

2 eggs

1 cup all-purpose flour

1 cup whole wheat flour

1 teaspoon baking powder

3 cups old-fashioned oats

$0.08 *per serving*

1 Heat oven to 350°F. In large bowl, beat brown sugar and butter with electric mixer on medium speed, scraping bowl occasionally, until light and fluffy. Beat in vanilla and eggs until well blended.

2 On low speed, beat in all-purpose flour, whole wheat flour and baking powder, scraping bowl occasionally, until well combined. Stir in oats.

3 On ungreased cookie sheet, drop dough by heaping tablespoonfuls 2 inches apart. Flatten cookies to about ¹/₂-inch thickness.

4 Bake 12 to 14 minutes or until light golden brown. Cool 1 minute; remove from cookie sheet to cooling racks.

1 Cookie: Calories 110; Total Fat 4.5g (Saturated Fat 2.5g, Trans Fat 0g); Cholesterol 20mg; Sodium 45mg; Total Carbohydrate 15g (Dietary Fiber 1g) **Exchanges:** 1 Other Carbohydrate, 1 Fat **Carbohydrate Choices:** 1

$mart $avings

No need to throw out that bag of brown sugar that's gotten hard. Just seal it in a plastic bag with an apple wedge for a day or two to soften, then throw away the apple.

Quick 'n Nutty Jam Gems

Only three ingredients, and you've filled your cookie jar with homemade cookies. These cookies are truly gems because they cost only $0.09 each!

Prep Time: 1 Hour 20 Minutes | **Start to Finish:** 1 Hour 20 Minutes | 4 dozen cookies

1 roll (16.5 oz) refrigerated sugar cookie dough

¾ cup finely chopped peanuts

⅓ cup strawberry jam or preserves

$0.09 *per serving*

1 Heat oven to 350°F. Cut cookie dough into 24 slices; cut each slice in half crosswise. Shape dough into balls and roll in peanuts. On ungreased cookie sheet, place 2 inches apart.

2 Bake 12 to 14 minutes or until edges are golden brown. Add heaping ¼ teaspoon jam. Remove from cookie sheet.

1 Cookie: Calories 60; Total Fat 3g (Saturated Fat 0.5g; Trans Fat 0.5g); Cholesterol 0mg; Sodium 40mg; Total Carbohydrate 8g (Dietary Fiber 0g) **Exchanges:** ½ Starch, ½ Fat **Carbohydrate Choices:** ½

$mart $avings

Plenty of jams and jellies on hand—apricot preserves, grape jelly, orange marmalade? Substitute any flavor you like for the strawberry, or use a variety to add color to your tray of cookies. And roll in any chopped nuts you have on hand, too. These easy colorful gems make a nice inexpensive gift.

Chunky Chocolate Cookies

Refrigerator cookie dough is great to have on hand to whip up a batch of cookies at a moment's notice. If you aren't a scratch baker, it will be less expensive to start with a roll of cookie dough than to buy all the ingredients for baking.

Prep Time: 25 Minutes | **Start to Finish:** 40 Minutes | 24 cookies

1 roll (16.5 oz) refrigerated sugar cookie dough

3 tablespoons unsweetened baking cocoa

1 cup semisweet chocolate chunks

½ cup miniature semisweet chocolate chips

½ cup chopped pecans

$0.28 *per serving*

1 Heat oven to 350°F. Into large bowl, break up cookie dough. Add remaining ingredients; mix well.

2 On ungreased cookie sheet, drop dough by well-rounded tablespoonfuls 2 inches apart.

3 Bake 8 to 11 minutes or just until set. Cool 2 minutes; remove from cookie sheet. Cool completely, about 15 minutes.

1 Cookie: Calories 160; Total Fat 9g (Saturated Fat 3g; Trans Fat 1g); Cholesterol 5mg; Sodium 65mg; Total Carbohydrate 19g (Dietary Fiber 1g) **Exchanges:** 1 ½ Other Carbohydrate, 1 ½ Fat **Carbohydrate Choices:** 1

$mart $avings

You can vary this cookie by substituting miniature candy-coated chocolate candies for the miniature chips and another favorite nut for the pecans. For a flavor change, stir in ½ cup of toffee bits, if you have them in the pantry, for the pecans.

METRIC CONVERSION GUIDE

VOLUME

U.S. Units	Canadian Metric	Australian Metric
¼ teaspoon	1 mL	1 ml
½ teaspoon	2 mL	2 ml
1 teaspoon	5 mL	5 ml
1 tablespoon	15 mL	20 ml
¼ cup	50 mL	60 ml
⅓ cup	75 mL	80 ml
½ cup	125 mL	125 ml
⅔ cup	150 mL	170 ml
¾ cup	175 mL	190 ml
1 cup	250 mL	250 ml
1 quart	1 liter	1 liter
1½ quarts	1.5 liters	1.5 liters
2 quarts	2 liters	2 liters
2½ quarts	2.5 liters	2.5 liters
3 quarts	3 liters	3 liters
4 quarts	4 liters	4 liters

WEIGHT

U.S. Units	Canadian Metric	Australian Metric
1 ounce	30 grams	30 grams
2 ounces	55 grams	60 grams
3 ounces	85 grams	90 grams
4 ounces (¼ pound)	115 grams	125 grams
8 ounces (½ pound)	225 grams	225 grams
16 ounces (1 pound)	455 grams	500 grams
1 pound	455 grams	0.5 kilogram

Note: The recipes in this cookbook have not been developed or tested using metric measures. When converting recipes to metric, some variations in quality may be noted.

MEASUREMENTS

Inches	Centimeters
1	2.5
2	5.0
3	7.5
4	10.0
5	12.5
6	15.0
7	17.5
8	20.5
9	23.0
10	25.5
11	28.0
12	30.5
13	33.0

TEMPERATURES

Fahrenheit	Celsius
32°	0°
212°	100°
250°	120°
275°	140°
300°	150°
325°	160°
350°	180°
375°	190°
400°	200°
425°	220°
450°	230°
475°	240°
500°	260°

Index

a

Alfredo Chicken Pasta, 14, 15
Appetizers
  as main meal, 185
  recipes for, 198–203, 206–215
Apple, Slices, Ham and Creamy Blue Cheese, 202
Artichoke-Spinach Strata, 154, 155
Asian Salmon, 140, 141
Asian Vegetable Stir-Fry, 174, 175
Asparagus, and Chicken Stir-Fry, 116, 117
Au Gratin Potatoes and Ham, 98, 99
Avocado, -Onion Slaw, Pulled Pork Sandwiches with, 102, 103

b

Bacon, and Tomatoes, Bow Ties with, 58, 59
Banana Boats, 204, 205
Banana Nut Energy Bars, 190, 191
Barbecue
  Chuck Roast, Grilled, 54
  Chuck Roast, Hoedown, 54, 55
  Pork Sandwiches, Easy, 100, 101
Barley
  -Lentil-Vegetable Skillet, 166, 167
  and Sweet Potato Risotto, 106, 107
Basil, -Tomato Soup, Chunky, 180, 181
Bean(s)
  and Cheese Nachos, Double, 172, 173
  Chili, Three-Bean, Smoky, 168, 169
  and Tuna Salad, Italian, 66, 67
  and Turkey, Tuscan, 72, 73
Beef. See also Burgers; Ground beef; Steak
  alternate cuts, trying, 13
  with Broccoli, 120, 121
  Chili, Chunky, 56, 57
  and Green Chile Enchiladas, 128, 129
  Gyro Pizza, 30
  Potato Nugget Casserole, 16
  -Ramen Soup, 28
  -Rice Burritos, 22
  Sandwiches, Hot Cheesy, 52, 53
  Skillet Supper, Sour Cream, 60, 61
  and Vegetable Chili, Chunky, 86, 87
  Vegetable Soup, 96, 97
Berry
  -Peach Smoothie, 195, 196
  -Strawberry Smoothie, 194

Biscuit, Cheeseburger Casserole, 34, 35
Blueberry, -Mango Smoothie, 192
Blue cheese
  Burgers, Grilled, 126, 127
  Creamy, and Ham Apple Slices, 202
  Creamy, and Prosciutto Pear Slices, 202, 203
Bow Ties with Bacon and Tomatoes, 58, 59
Broccoli, Beef with, 120, 121
Broiled Lemon-Thyme Tuna Steaks, 144, 145
Brown Sugar–Oatmeal Cookies, 216, 217
Bruschetta-Style Tortellini Salad, 62, 63
Budget, food, 6
Bulk purchase, 9
Burgers
  Blue Cheese, Grilled, 126, 127
  Shanghai Sliders, 124, 125
Burritos
  Beef Rice, 22
  Chicken-Rice, 22, 23
  Egg, Scrambled, 156, 157
  Pork-Rice, 22

c

Casserole(s)
  Beef Potato Nugget, 16, 17
  Chicken and Rice, 78, 79
  Chicken Potato Nugget, 16, 17
  Crescent-Topped Ratatouille, 176, 177
  freezing, 9
Cheese
  and Bean Nachos, Double, 172, 173
  and Chile Empanaditas, 214, 215
  Chili Mac 'n, 38, 39
  Four-, Pasta, 130, 131
  as meat substitute, 149
  -Stuffed Pepperoni Pizza, 136, 137
  -and Vegetable-Stuffed Shells, 160, 161
Cheeseburger Casserole, Biscuit, 34, 35
Cheeseburger Pizza, 46, 47
Cheeseburger Tacos, 50, 51
Cheesy
  Baked Supper Omelet, 152, 153
  Chicken-Tortilla Lasagna, 24
  Chicken Tortilla Lasagna, 25
  Hot Beef Sandwiches, 52, 53
  Rounds, Onion-Mushroom Soup with, 182, 183

Chex® Muddy Buddies®, 188, 189
Chicago Deep-Dish Sausage Pizza, 134, 135
Chicken
  Alfredo Pasta, 14, 15
  alternate cuts, trying, 13
  and Asparagus Stir-Fry, 116, 117
  Chili, White, 20, 21
  Divan Crescent Squares, 64
  Divan Skillet, 110, 111
  and Noodles, Thai Peanut, 118, 119
  Potato Nugget Casserole, 16, 17
  Pot Pie, Skillet, 18, 19
  Pot Roast Dinner, 74, 75
  -Ramen Soup, 28, 29
  -Rice Burritos, 22, 23
  and Rice Casserole, 78, 79
  rotisserie, price value of, 11
  Saltimbocca, 114, 115
  Sandwiches, Grilled Fiesta, 112, 113
  Summer Soup, with Biscuit Dumplings, 26, 27
  -Tortilla Lasagna, Cheesy, 24, 25
  Tortilla Soup, 76, 77
Chick Pea and Tomato Curry, 170, 171
Chile and Cheese Empanaditas, 214, 215
Chili
  Beef, Chunky, 56, 57
  Beef and Vegetable, Chunky, 86, 87
  Chicken, White, 20, 21
  Mac 'n Cheese, 38, 39
  Three-Bean, Smoky, 168, 169
Chipotle Butter, Grilled Halibut with, 142, 143
Chocolate, Cookies, Chunky, 220, 221
Chowder, Edamame Corn, 178, 179
Chunky Beef and Vegetable Chili, 86, 87
Chunky Beef Chili, 56, 57
Chunky Chocolate Cookies, 220, 221
Chunky Tomato-Basil Soup, 180, 181
Community Supported Agriculture (CSA), 8
Cookies
  Brown Sugar–Oatmeal, 216, 217
  Chunky Chocolate, 220, 221
  Quick 'n Nutty Jam Gems, 218, 219
Corn
  Edamame Chowder, 178, 179
  -Topped Potato Skins, Ground Beef and, 42, 43
Coupons, 7

Crescent Squares, Tuna Divan, 64, *65*
Crescent-Topped Ratatouille Casserole, 176, *177*
Curry/Curried
    Chick Pea and Tomato, 170, *171*
    Lentil Soup, 104, *105*

d

Deviled Eggs, Ranch, 206, *207*
Dilly Veggie Dip, 200, *201*
Dining out
    cost-saving tips, 109
    at home, recipes for, 110–147
Dipping Sticks, Pizza, 212, *213*
Dips
    Dilly Veggie, 200, *201*
    Red Pepper Hummus, 198, *199*
Double Cheese and Bean Nachos, 172, *173*
Double-Meat Personal Pizza, 48, *49*
Dumplings, Biscuit, Chicken Summer Soup
    with, 26, *27*

e

Easy Barbecue Pork Sandwiches, 100, *101*
Edamame Corn Chowder, 178, *179*
Egg(s)
    Burritos, Scrambled, 156, *157*
    Deviled, Ranch, 206, *207*
    dinner options with, 149
    recipes with, 150–159
    -Vegetable Bake, Make-Ahead, 150, *151*
Empanaditas, Cheese and Chile, 214, *215*
Enchiladas
    Beef and Green Chile, 128, *129*
    Mexican Rice, No-Roll, 164, *165*
Energy Bars, Banana Nut, 190, *191*
Everyday Lasagna Skillet, 32, *33*

f

Farm-grown food, sources for, 8
Fish. *See also* Halibut; Salmon; Tuna
    less-expensive types, 13
    Tacos, 146, *147*
Food cost savings
    big-batch cooking, 10, 185
    bulk purchase, 9
    dining out at home tips, 109
    farm-grown/local goods, buying, 8, 13
    and food budget, 6
    food waste, avoiding, 9
    freezing, tips for, 9, 10
    for kitchen organizational products, 8
    leftovers, tips for, 10
    master grocery list for, 6
    and meal-planning, 6–7, 10

one-time ingredients, using again, 11
organizing kitchen for, 9
Pantry Cookoff versus takeout, 9
price check notebook, 6
shopping, planning for, 7
and slow cooker, 69
in-supermarket tips, 8
time versus money situations, 9
unit price per ounce, calculating, 7
Four-Cheese Pasta, 130, *131*
Freezing
    casseroles, 9
    tips for, 10
French Dip Sandwiches, 84, *85*
French Onion Beef Steak, 90, *91*
Frittata, Vegetable, 158, *159*

g

Gardening, produce, container gardening, 8
Garden Vegetable Lasagna, 162, *163*
Goulash, Mom's Skillet, 36, *37*
Green chiles
    and Beef Enchiladas, 128, *129*
    and Cheese Empanaditas, 214, *215*
Grilled Blue Cheese Burgers, 126, *127*
Grilled Fiesta Chicken Sandwiches, 112, *113*
Grilled Flank Steak Salad with Parmesan
    Crisps, 122, *123*
Grilled Halibut with Chipotle Butter, 142, *143*
Grilled Hoedown BBQ Chuck Roast, 54
Grilled Lemon-Thyme Tuna Steaks, 144, *145*
Grocery list, 6
Ground beef. *See also* Burgers; Chili
    Biscuit Cheeseburger Casserole, 34, *35*
    Cheeseburger Pizza, 46, *47*
    Cheeseburger Tacos, 50, *51*
    Cheesy Hot Beef Sandwiches, 52, *53*
    Chili Mac 'n Cheese, 38, *39*
    and Corn-Topped Potato Skins, 42, *43*
    Double-Meat Personal Pizza, 48, *49*
    Mom's Skillet Goulash, 36, *37*
    Pizza Skillet Hot Dish, 44, *45*
    Shanghai Sliders, 124, *125*
    Slow-Simmered Meat Sauce, Spaghetti
        with, 80, *81*
    and Vegetable Noodle Dinner, 40, *41*
Gyro
    Pizza, Beef, 30
    Pizza, Turkey, 30, *31*

h

Halibut, Grilled, with Chipotle Butter, 142, *143*
Ham
    and Creamy Blue Cheese Apple Slices, 202
    and Potatoes Au Gratin, 98, *99*

Happy hour
    food specials with, 109
    at home, 109
Herbs, fresh, storing, 149
Hoedown BBQ Chuck Roast, 54, *55*
Hummus, Red Pepper, 198, *199*

i

Italian Bean and Tuna Salad, 66, *67*

k

Key lime, –Strawberry Smoothie, 194, *195*

l

Lamb, alternate cuts, trying, 13
Lasagna
    Chicken-Tortilla, Cheesy, 24, *25*
    Garden Vegetable, 162, *163*
    Skillet, Everyday, 32, *33*
Leftovers
    as appetizers, 185
    and cost savings, 6, 10
Lemon
    -Thyme Tuna Steaks, Broiled, 144
    -Thyme Tuna Steaks, Grilled, 144, *145*
Lentil
    Lentil-Barley-Vegetable Skillet, 166, *167*
    Soup, Curried, 104, *105*

m

Make-Ahead Vegetable-Egg Bake, 150, *151*
Mango, -Blueberry Smoothie, 192
Meal-planning, 6–7
Meat
    cost-saving tips, 13
    stretching, recipes for, 14–67
Meatless dishes
    recipes for, 150–183
    tips for, 149
Melon-Raspberry Smoothies, 192, *193*
Mom's Skillet Goulash, 36, *37*
Mostaccioli with Italian Sausage, 132, *133*
Mushroom, -Onion Soup with Cheesy Rounds,
    182, *183*

n

Nachos, Cheese and Bean, Double, 172, *173*
Noodle(s)
    and Chicken, Thai Peanut, 118, *119*
    Dinner, Beef and Vegetable, 40, *41*
No-Roll Mexican Rice Enchiladas, 164, *165*

o

Oatmeal, –Brown Sugar Cookies, 216, *217*
Omelet, Cheesy Baked Supper, 152, *153*

Onion, -Mushroom Soup with Cheesy Rounds, *183*

Onion(s)
-Avocado Slaw, Pulled Pork Sandwiches with, 102, *103*
Beef Steak, Onion, 90, *91*
-Mushroom Soup with Cheesy Rounds, 182

On-the-Go Pepperoni Pizzas, 210, *211*

Orange, Double, -Strawberry Smoothie, 194

p

Parmesan Crisps, Grilled Flank Steak Salad with, 122, *123*

Party Snack Mix, 186, *187*

Pasta
Alfredo Chicken, 14, *15*
Four-Cheese, 130, *131*

Peach
-Berry Smoothie, 196, *197*
-Strawberry Smoothie, 194

Peanut, Thai, Chicken and Noodles, 118, *119*

Pear, Slices, Prosciutto and Creamy Blue Cheese, 202, *203*

Pepperoni
Cheese-Stuffed Pizza, 136, *137*
Pizza, On-the-Go, 210, *211*

Pizza
Beef Gyro, 30
Cheeseburger, 46, *47*
Dipping Sticks, 212, *213*
Double-Meat Personal, 48, *49*
Pepperoni, On-the-Go, 210, *211*
Pepperoni Cheese-Stuffed, 136, *137*
Sausage, Chicago Deep Dish, 134, *135*
Skillet Hot Dish, 44, *45*
Turkey Gyro, 30, *31*

Pork
alternate cuts, trying, 13
Pulled, Sandwiches with Avocado-Onion Slaw, 102, *103*
-Rice Burritos, 22
Sandwiches, Easy Barbecue, 100, *101*

Potato(es)
Beef Nugget Casserole, 16
Chicken Nugget Casserole, 16, *17*
and Ham Au Gratin, 98, *99*
Skins, Corn-Topped, Ground Beef and, 42, *43*

Potluck parties, 109, 185

Pot Pie, Chicken Skillet, 18, *19*

Pot Roast
Chicken Dinner, 74, *75*
with Creamy Dill Sauce, 82, *83*
Steak and Vegetables, 94, *95*

Proscuitto and Creamy Blue Cheese Pear Slices, 202, *203*

Pulled Pork Sandwiches with Avocado-Onion Slaw, 102, *103*

q

Quick 'n Nutty Jam Gems, 218, *219*

r

Ramen
-Beef Soup, 28
-Chicken Soup, 28, *29*

Ranch Deviled Eggs, 206, *207*

Raspberry, -Melon Smoothies, 192, *193*

Ratatouille, Casserole, Crescent-Topped, 176, *177*

Red Pepper Hummus, 198, *199*

Rice
-Beef Burritos, 22
-Chicken Burritos, *22, 23*
and Chicken Casserole, 78, *79*
Mexican, Enchiladas, No-Roll, 164, *165*
-Pork Burritos, 22

Risotto, Barley and Sweet Potato, 106, *107*

Roll-Ups, Turkey Dijon, 208, *209*

Round Steak Stroganoff, 92, *93*

s

Salad(s)
Bruschetta-Style Tortellini, 62, *63*
Grilled Flank Steak, with Parmesan Crisps, 122, *123*
Italian Bean and Tuna, 66, *67*

Salmon, Asian, 140, *141*

Saltimbocca, Chicken, 114, *115*

Sandwiches
Barbecue Pork, Easy, 100, *101*
Beef, Hot, Cheesy, 52, *53*
French Dip, 84, *85*
Grilled Chicken Fiesta, 112, *113*

Sausage
Italian, Mostaccioli with, 132, *133*
Pizza, Chicago Deep-Dish, 134, *135*

Scrambled Egg Burritos, 156, *157*

Seafood. *See* Shrimp

Shanghai Sliders, 124, *125*

Shrimp Scampi, 138, *139*

Skillet dishes
Beef Supper, Sour Cream, 60, *61*
Chicken Divan, 110, *111*
Chicken Pot Pie, 18, *19*
Goulash, Mom's, 36, *37*
Hot Dish, Pizza, 44, *45*
Lasagna, Everyday, 32, *33*
Lentil-Barley-Vegetable, 166, *167*

Slaw, Avocado-Onion, Pulled Pork Sandwiches with, 102, *103*

Sliders, Shanghai, 124, *125*

Slow cooker
and cost savings, 69
features, selecting, 69
lid, keeping in place while cooking, 69
recipes, 70–107

Smoky Three-Bean Chili, 168, *169*

Smoothies
Blueberry-Mango, 192
Melon-Raspberry, 192, *193*
Peach-Berry, 196, *197*
Strawberry-Berry, 194
Strawberry–Double Orange, 194
Strawberry–Key Lime, 194, *195*
Strawberry-Peach, 194

Smothered Swiss Steak, 88, *89*

Snack(s)
big-batch, repackaging, 185
cost-saving tips, 185
Party Mix, 186, *187*
recipes for, 186–221

Soup
Beef-Ramen, 28
Chicken-Ramen, 28, *29*
Chicken Summer, with Biscuit Dumplings, 26, *27*
Chicken Tortilla, 76, *77*
Curried Lentil, 104, *105*
Onion-Mushroom, with Cheesy Rounds, 182, *183*
Tomato-Basil, Chunky, 180, *181*
Vegetable Beef, 96, *97*

Sour Cream Beef Skillet Supper, 60, *61*

Spaghetti with Slow-Simmered Meat Sauce, 80, *81*

Spices, storing, 149

Spinach, -Artichoke Strata, 154, *155*

Steak
Grilled Flank Salad, with Parmesan Crisps, 122, *123*
Round, Stroganoff, 92, *93*
Steak, French Onion, 90, *91*
Swiss, Smothered, 88, *89*
and Vegetables Pot Roast, 94, *95*

Stir-Fry
Chicken and Asparagus, 116, *117*
Vegetable, Asian, 174, *175*

Strata, Artichoke-Spinach, 154, *155*

Strawberry
-Berry Smoothie, 194
–Double Orange Smoothie, 194
–Key Lime Smoothie, 194, *195*
-Peach Smoothie, 194

Stroganoff, Round Steak, 92, *93*
Stuffed Shells, Cheese-and Vegetable-, 160, *161*
Summer Chicken Soup with Biscuit Dumplings, 26, *27*
Sweet Potato, and Barley Risotto, 106, *107*
Swiss Steak, Smothered, 88, *89*

t

Tacos
    Cheeseburger, 50, *51*
    Fish, 146, *147*
Takeout, avoiding, 9
Thai Peanut Chicken and Noodles, 118, *119*
Tomato(es)
    and Bacon, Bow Ties with, 58, *59*
    -Basil Soup, Chunky, 180, *181*
    and Chick Pea Curry, 170, *171*
Tortellini, Salad, Bruschetta-Style, 62, *63*

Tortilla
    -Chicken Lasagna, Cheesy, 24, *25*
    Chicken Soup, 76, *77*
Tuna
    and Bean Salad, Italian, 66, *67*
    Steaks, Broiled Lemon-Thyme, 144
    Steaks, Grilled Lemon-Thyme, 144, *145*
Tuna Divan Crescent Squares, 64, *65*
Turkey
    and Beans, Tuscan, 72, *73*
    Breast with Vegetables, 70, *71*
    Dijon Roll-Ups, 208, *209*
    Gyro Pizza, 30, *31*
Tuscan Turkey and Beans, 72, *73*

u

Unit price per ounce, calculating, 7

v

Vegetable(s)
    and Beef Chili, Chunky, 86, *87*
    and Beef Noodle Dinner, 40, *41*
    Beef Soup, 96, *97*
    -and Cheese Stuffed Shells, 160, *161*
    Dip, Dilly, 200, *201*
    -Egg Bake, Make-Ahead, 150, *151*
    Frittata, 158, *159*
    Lasagna, Garden, 162, *163*
    -Lentil-Barley Skillet, 166, *167*
    and Steak Pot Roast, 94, *95*
    Stir-Fry, Asian, 174, *175*
    Turkey Breast with, 70, *71*

w

White Chicken Chili, 20, *21*

Hungry for more?
See what else
Pillsbury has to offer.

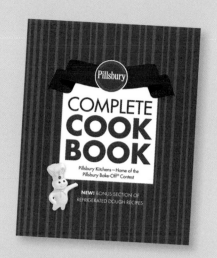

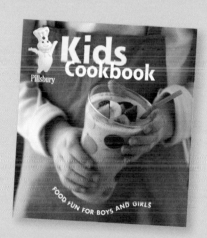